THE AMERICAN HIGH SCHOOL
AND THE TALENTED STUDENT

The American High School and the  Talented Student

by FRANK O. COPLEY

Foreword by Richard Pearson

ANN ARBOR

THE UNIVERSITY OF MICHIGAN PRESS

FOREWORD

Today, without much fanfare, but with heartening effectiveness, the American high school is responding to the recent flow of criticism directed at the nation's educational system. This book, by Professor Frank O. Copley, reports such a response. Professor Copley's focus is the instruction of the academically talented student of high-school age—the confrontation between such a student and an experienced teacher. His environment is the comprehensive high school in all its variety, from the small rural school with limited resources to the wealthy suburban school. His approach is conservative. His conclusions are hopeful, and they carry conviction because they rest upon direct observation of what some high schools in Michigan are now doing.

The background for the present report is the series of three notable experiments sponsored by the Fund for the Advancement of Education, beginning in 1953 and 1954, a year or more before Sputnik I. One of these, a Study of General Education in School and College, documented the waste and duplication that occur when strong schools offer challenging programs for able students and when these efforts are not articulated with the work of the first two years of college. The second study dealt with early admission to college and showed that, given the right circumstances, able students could enter college a year or two early and successfully undertake the academic work. Early admission, however, misjudged the mood of the high schools. It failed to recognize that the schools were not willing to admit their inability to deal with able students, because they depended upon them to set the pace for the rest of the students. This position of the high schools was reinforced by the finding from the early admission study which revealed that academic talent and emotional maturity do not always develop at an even rate. There were good grounds to believe that the place for the able student of high-school age was in school, with other students of his own age.

The strong reaction against early admission led to the formation of the third study sponsored by the Fund: the School and College Study of Admission with Advanced Standing. This study and its successor, the Advanced Placement Program, rest on the belief that schools could, if they would, offer work of college caliber; that able students could handle such work in the twelfth grade and, occasionally, earlier; and that schools and colleges together could devise the mechanisms to get the job done in the schools and get it recognized in the colleges.

The Advanced Placement Program has since come under the sponsorship of the College Entrance Examination Board as an ongoing activity. It gained acceptance in the schools and colleges because it had the support of experienced teachers at both levels. Professor Copley's report symbolizes the central role of the teacher in Advanced Placement. It also adds to the growing evidence that this approach can be made a part of the philosophy and the practice of the comprehensive high school.

Academic talent is by no means an unknown quantity

to the experienced teacher. He deals with it every day and has developed an outlook and some rules of thumb which, by and large, work pretty well. It is true that the experienced teacher often has had to improvise; he couldn't always wait for the latest research findings. He often has had to make do with inadequate resources; he didn't always have the patience to induce reluctant school boards to spend more money than they wanted to. He often has found himself relegated to the background of public discussions about education; he didn't really want to leave the classroom for the political arena. And it is unhappily true that the experienced teacher was all too often concerned with his own classroom, not that of his colleague in a neighboring school or college. But most of all, the experienced teacher has had to face talented students regularly and directly. He has had no alternative but to develop an outlook and a *modus operandi,* and that's what this book is about.

Professor Copley is an experienced teacher. He teaches Latin, but he took a year off to study the talented student and how he fares today in the American high school. His report is a synthesis of scholarship on the psychology of the talented and of direct observation in a variety of schools. To this synthesis he has added a large measure of his own teaching experience.

This is a practical book. It starts with a discussion of the educational issues surrounding the academically talented: who they are, how to identify them, whether to provide them with enrichment, acceleration, or both, and how to group them according to ability. Each of these topics is examined with the teacher in mind and with generous allowance for the variety that exists among students, schools, and subjects.

The second half of the book offers some shrewd advice about starting and maintaining a program of Advanced Placement: how to find the right teacher, how to organize the courses, how to utilize available resources, and how to take account of the school's size. It warns of such pitfalls as variation in college practice in the award of course credit, unrealistic grading systems, and undue reliance upon standardized tests. It considers the idiosyncrasies of the various subject disciplines and the extent to which each can be made to fit the general Advanced Placement approach.

Withal, this is not a "how-to-do-it" book. No pat formulas are given: instead, the issues and problems are laid out and the alternatives discussed. The reader will have to supply his own answers.

It would be wrong to be misled by the practical organization and approach of Professor Copley's report. We remarked earlier that the experienced teacher had *both* an outlook and a *modus operandi* in dealing with able students. It is likely that the outlook is the more important of the two; certainly, it has implications for a variety of practices and for selecting among them.

This author's outlook is defined largely by example and comment as he discusses the practical applications. He holds some firm opinions about education and the art of teaching and he does not hesitate to express them. There is a pointed essay on the teaching of "critical thinking"; it is too often, he thinks, taught without reference to challenging subject matter, yet it can only be taught with such a reference. There is disagreement with Mr. Conant's judgment about the capacity of the small rural high school to deal with the able student. Professor Copley feels this judgment is too harsh, and we know this is because he has seen strong teaching and eager learning in this environment. There is some disillusionment with the growing specialization of guidance. In all likelihood, this can be traced to dissatisfaction with any group which threatens a monopoly on wisdom and a corner on good advice.

The outlook is also defined by the topics the author chooses not to develop or comment upon. Administrative questions are treated lightly or ignored entirely, perhaps because of the teacher's confidence in administrators when they confine themselves to administration. The reader will not find a careful accounting of the dollars-and-cents cost of working with talented students. Probably Professor Copley would consider such precision superfluous; the important thing is to strike a balance between the cost of this work and the cost of wasted talent. The author leaves little doubt where he thinks the greater cost lies. In a similar fashion, educational research is treated with understanding and respect, but also gingerly and with no more emphasis than is absolutely necessary.

This, then, is the outlook of the teacher who believes it is high time to bring the argument right into the classroom and who has faith in the learning experience and in curious youth. The hopeful thing about this outlook is that it was confirmed by a year's scholarship and visitation. We are not out of the woods by any manner of means and this book does not contain the final answer. We are, however, making progress with talented students and this chiefly because the country's experienced teachers, like Professor Copley, are attending to their profession. Our prayer should be that there are enough such teachers.

RICHARD PEARSON
Executive Vice President,
College Entrance Examination Board
New York, N.Y.

PREFACE

For a number of years now, the interest of educators at all levels in the United States has been focused on the problem of providing an education for the superior student that would be at once better adapted to his needs and more immediately responsive to the requirements of present-day society. At the University of Michigan, in the College of Literature, Science, and the Arts, this interest led, in 1957, to the establishment of an Honors Program, running throughout the four college years, to which freshmen are admitted on the basis of high school records and test scores. The program involves special honors sections of large freshman and sophomore courses, as well as interdisciplinary seminars.

The College was well aware of the experimental nature of its program; equally, it was deeply conscious of the fact that its work, far from being an isolated part of the educational process, was intimately connected with the preparatory functions of the secondary and elementary schools. Accordingly, in 1958, application was made to the Carnegie Corporation of New York for funds to strengthen programs for superior students both at the high school and at the college level. The study at the College was directed by Dr. Robert C. Angell, professor of sociology and director of the Honors Program; I was asked to carry on the work with the secondary schools, with the proviso that I would be granted a leave of absence for this purpose from February 1959 to September 1960.

It was my understanding that I was "to advise and consult with the high schools of Michigan on programs of study for superior students." For this rather impressive assignment I could present only the most general qualifications: some twenty-seven years of college teaching, four years as adviser to freshmen and sophomores, and some scattered years as departmental adviser to juniors, seniors, and graduate students; five years as director of admissions with advanced standing; and a lifelong interest in students and their problems. With the technical aspects of education and the writings of the professional educators I had almost no acquaintance; I could claim no understanding of research methods in this field. Under the circumstances the only approach open to me was the purely practical one: I could try to find out what had been done, and pass this on, with such additions and elaborations as might grow out of my own educational experience, to any school that was interested. I could make myself available for questioning; I could attempt to arouse interest where interest was lacking, and encourage it where it already existed. Finally, I could bring to the high schools of Michigan the assurance that the faculty of the College of Literature, Science, and the Arts was interested in their problems and concerned to work with them toward improving the educational system of the state.

During the fall semester of 1958–59 and throughout the period of my assignment, I spent such free time as was available to me in a study of some of the literature on the education of the talented student. Beginning with Terman's *Genetic Studies of Genius* and Terman and Oden's *The*

Gifted Child Grows Up, I made my way through a rather random collection of books, pamphlets, and newspaper and journal articles, many of them of a popular rather than a professional cast.* Such parts of this as proved helpful to me in establishing specific points will be referred to in the notes. I might mention here, besides the Terman studies, such books as James B. Conant, *The American High School Today* and *id., The Child, the Parent, and the State;* Paul Woodring, *Fourth of a Nation;* Passow, Goldberg, Tannenbaum, and French, *Planning for Talented Youth;* the Harvard report, *General Education in a Free Society;* the report of the National Society for the Study of Education, *Education for the Gifted* (1958); and for the views of a layman, critical but not ill-tempered, John Keats, *Schools without Scholars.* The substance of my report is based partly on this unsystematic reading, partly on my own experiences as teacher, adviser, and administrator, but most largely on the conferences that I was privileged to hold with literally hundreds of my fellow teachers in the elementary and high schools during my tour of duty. To the teachers, guidance officers, principals, and superintendents who so patiently listened to me and who taught me far more than I taught them, I am deeply grateful. Without their help my work could never have been done; this report represents in large degree the essence of what I learned from them.

In order to get the project under way, Professor Angell, early in March 1959, sent a letter to all the accredited high

---

* I have not felt it worth while to make a bibliography of these writings, since much of what I read proved too imprecise or too tendentious to be truly useful. Bibliographies on the subject of the gifted child are available from the NEA Academically Talented Student Project, 1201 Sixteenth Street, N.W., Washington 6, D.C.

schools of Michigan, informing them of the nature of the project and of the fact that I was available to visit their institutions and to discuss the problem of education for the superior student with teachers, administrators, students, PTA or other parents' organizations, curriculum study groups, and the like. In the meantime, in order to observe and study programs that were already in operation, I asked and was readily granted permission to visit Ann Arbor High School, Tappan Junior High School, Burns Park Elementary School, Mumford and Denby high schools in Detroit, Evanston Township High School, Evanston, Illinois, and New Trier High School, Winnetka, Illinois. In these schools I spent from one to four days visiting classes and conferring with teachers, students, and administrators. These visits, together with such preliminary reading as I had been able to do, provided the foundation for my subsequent work; the programs that I found in successful operation became the models on which I based my activities as consultant.

In response to Professor Angell's letter I received about twenty invitations from the schools; altogether in the spring semester of 1959 I made visits to twenty-five schools, plus a few talks to nonschool groups such as the Kiwanis Club. In May, I sent out a follow-up letter to the schools from which no reply had been received; response to this second letter provided me with engagements throughout the fall semester and on into the spring semester of 1959–60. Toward the end of this year I supplemented the invitations with visits to other schools that had been reported to me as having particularly successful programs for their abler students. Altogether, including all school visits and all meetings, conferences, etc., I fulfilled 124 engagements. The schools visited ranged from large city institutions to crossroads schools hardly more than a step removed from the country schoolhouse. Ordinarily I was invited to address a teachers' meeting at which all members of the staff of the school were present. Less frequently I met with department heads, administrative and guidance officers, curriculum committees, citizens' committees, and PTA or other service groups. In virtually every instance I was received with the greatest cordiality; interest in my project was evinced by question sessions that often ran well over an hour and all too frequently left me very near the end of my stock of answers. I think it may be categorically stated that the high schools of Michigan are acutely conscious of the need for programs that will adequately meet the educational requirements of the students of exceptional ability, that they are equally conscious of the inadequacies of current school programs in this respect, and that they are warmly receptive to all offers of assistance, particularly from college teachers in the so-called "subject matter" fields.

I should like to express my gratitude to Professor Angell and the Honors Council of the College of Literature, Science, and the Arts, and through them to the Carnegie Corporation of New York for the grant that made my project possible. Professor Angell also deserves my sincerest thanks for his invaluable advice and for the unfailing kindness and patience with which he gave it. I am further indebted to Dr. Clyde Vroman, director of admissions at the University, for allowing me to draw on his enormous store of information about the schools of Michigan, to Dr. Ray E. Kehoe, of the Bureau of School Services, for his help in making contacts with many schools and for his wise and friendly counsel, and to Professor C. F. Lehmann, of the School of Education, for directing my attention to particularly fruitful areas of study and for his help in avoiding the pitfalls into which professors of the liberal arts are likely to fall when they venture into the terra incognita of professional pedagogy. I owe especial thanks to Mr. Anthony Kallet, a graduate student in psychology at the University of Michigan, for generously giving me the benefit of his understanding of the psychology of talented children.

As for people in the schools, when one owes so much to so many, it is hard to single out any for specific mention; it is fair to say that I learned something from every teacher and administrator with whom I talked. Still my special thanks go to Mr. Nicholas Schreiber, principal, Ann Arbor High School; to Mr. Gene D. Maybee, principal, Tappan Junior High School, Ann Arbor; to Miss Marion Cranmore, principal, Burns Park School, Ann Arbor; to Mr. Robert Granville and Mr. Frank Reed, of the English department of Ann Arbor High School; to Mr. Clarence W. Hach, head of the English department of Evanston Township High School; to Mr. R. H. Carpenter, dean of the faculty of New Trier High School; to Mr. M. M. Gillender, principal, Godwin Heights High School, Grand Rapids; to Mr. B. J. McCormick, principal, Allderdice High School, Pittsburgh, Pa.; to Dr. Edwin A. Fenton, of Allderdice High School and Carnegie Institute of Technology; to Dr. Mary Sheehan, principal, and Dr. Lenoir H. Burnside, psychologist, of Monroe High School, Rochester, N.Y. These men and women gave me hours of their valuable time and much advice and information that could not have been obtained elsewhere; from all of them I learned a new and abiding respect for the teachers and administrators of our schools.

Finally, because the Advanced Placement Program seems to me to figure so largely in any thinking about the education of the superior student, I should like to express my appreciation for valuable assistance to Mr. S. A. Kendrick, vice-president, CEEB; to Mr. Jack N. Arbolino, director of the Advanced Placement Program; to Mr. John R. Valley, of ETS; to Mr. E. G. Wilcox, director of Advanced Placement, Harvard University; and to Mr. Charles Keller, formerly director of the A.P.P., now director of the John Hay Fellows Program.

FRANK O. COPLEY
Professor of Latin and
Consultant to High Schools,
Literary College Honors Project

CONTENTS

I

ACCELERATION,
ENRICHMENT,
AND ABILITY GROUPING

Dr. James B. Conant, at the outset of his book, *The Child, the Parent, and the State*, confesses to a "sense of distasteful weariness" that overtakes him "when someone writes or says that what we need . . . is to decide first what we mean by the word 'education.'" Most teachers will know exactly what Dr. Conant is talking about; few disciplines are so obsessed with definitions as is the one that years ago dropped a distinctive and useful name, "Pedagogy," for the vague and misleading one of "Education." Today, the educational theorists, in their writing and speaking, frequently become so entangled in definitions that they fail to come to grips with issues at all. At other times, having fastened on a definition that seems workable, they erect upon it an argument that may be a model of objectivity but will always remain unconvincing to those who regard the basic definition as inexact, incomplete, or otherwise unsatisfactory.[1] And since education (not Education) is a human phenomenon, and since it is unlikely that any definition of a human phenomenon will ever win universal acceptance, it looks as if this bewildering farrago of embattled definitions and unresolved issues is to be with us, world without end.

If Education were a remote, academic subject like Assyriology or the higher reaches of metaphysics, no one would mind. The truths of Assyriology are important, as are all truths, and the correct resolution of a problem in cuneiform is a legitimate concern of the scholar, but if no resolution be found, or an incorrect one accepted, most of us will not be seriously affected. The trouble is that Education deals with education, and education affects you and me, your child and my child; it affects the intellectual and the moral climate of society; it may even be a critical element in our survival as a nation. If education must wait until Education has completed its search for definitions, then something rather worse than Conant's "sense of distasteful weariness" is likely to overtake us. The search must go on, and those of us who stand outside Education could afford to learn a little humility as we watch our colleagues struggle with complex problems of human behavior: are we so much wiser than the "Educationists," or is it just that the definitions we seek are either easier to find or somewhat less vital? There is only one demand that we may legitimately make, and that is that until ultimate definitions are found, practical rules of thumb and the wisdom of experience be allowed to operate; that working teachers and concerned citizens be listened to with respect, and not brushed aside as mere laymen or "naïve observers"; and that attempts to improve education be not put off "until needed research is complete." [2] This would appear to be the substance of Conant's plea: that we who are concerned with the here and now of education put aside the search for premises and definitions and consider instead what is going on in our schools and colleges, and what skilled and experienced teachers on all levels might do to improve them.[3]

Consonant with this plea, I shall not attempt here to arrive at a final and objective definition of the superior student, but shall limit myself to what we know from experience about him. Very nearly the first thing we discover is that he is almost never called "superior." School people view the term as invidious and undemocratic. They also complain of its inexactitude: it is too broad and general, they say, for there are many kinds of superiority and we do not know which kind is meant. The twin desires for a more palatable and for a more precise term have led to the use of "gifted," "talented," "able and ambitious," and the like. These are not very satisfactory either, since there are as many kinds of gifts and talents as there are of superiority, and while "able" is a harmless term, "ambitious" can be nearly as invidious as "superior" itself. Educational literature is of very little help here. Some writers distinguish between "gifted" and "talented" in terms of IQ, the "talented" ranging, e.g., from 120 to 135 and the "gifted" from 135 up; others use "gifted" to mean those who excel in academic subjects, and "talented" those whose excellence shows itself in music or the arts; still others reverse these roles. Others, finally, lump the terms together, using them quite interchangeably to refer to that segment of the school population which in their estimation is "superior" in one way or another. This last group likes to think of superiority in terms of percentages: they will declare the top 5, 10, 15, or even 25 per cent of the school population to be "superior" (or "gifted" or "talented" or "able and ambitious," as the case may be). It is small wonder that one educator remarked rather wistfully, "Our information on the characteristics of the intellectually able child is fairly adequate, but our ability to identify him still lacks precision." [4]

Where even the experts disagree, I shall certainly not attempt a solution. Of all the names invented for the superior student, "academically talented," the one preferred by Conant, seems to me to be as near to precise as possible; it clearly suggests superior ability in the familiar old-line disciplines: English, mathematics, the foreign languages, history, and the physical and natural sciences. If we think of our superior students as almost without exception college-bound, or even graduate school–bound, then these are the kinds of superiority that will count the most.[5] Whenever possible, I shall use Conant's term but shall not hesitate to use "gifted" or "talented," "able and ambitious" or even "superior," if the exigencies of style demand it; for the purposes of this report, these terms are to be regarded as synonymous.

Granted this imprecision in terminology, we are still faced with the problem of a working definition: who are these students whom we are to call, variously, "talented," "gifted," etc.? Let me state it first in terms of rough guideposts, and then see if later on we can be more precise. For this report I should say that academic talent begins at about IQ 120 or 125, or, in terms of the College Entrance Examination Board's Scholastic Aptitude Tests (commonly referred to as CEEB SAT), at a score of about 620, both verbal and quantitative. In national percentages it falls in the top 5 per cent of the high school population. These are only the roughest sort of indicators, and none of them should be used alone; the tests, however excellent, are not that good as yet.

Still sound, and by many educators regarded as quite definitive, are grades earned in school in academic subjects. Here there is, of course, enormous variation; it is an elementary educational fact that an A at school X is a C at school Y. Nevertheless, ratings based on grades have a strange way of being about as accurate as any others, and they have the vast merit of being readily available. When we speak of the academically talented in terms of grades, we mean those students whose grades in academic subjects fall consistently

in the A to B range, who rarely get C's, and almost never a
D or an E. Here again we must watch for variation; too
great an insistence on consistency and uniform excellence
may lead us to pass by many a youngster whose gifts are
definitely, sometimes even grotesquely, lopsided.

IQ of about 120 or better, SAT scores in the 600's, grades
consistently A's and B's—leaven this statistical lump with the
opinions of wise and experienced teachers and advisers, and
we shall have something resembling a working criterion of
"academic talent." Probably the one mistake that must be
avoided at all costs is rigidity, for although the academically
talented have some characteristics in common, they are also
subject to wide variation.[6] Some have many interests; some
concentrate all their energies on one. Some are well-
adjusted, some are miserably ill-adjusted—and I suspect that
we had better think carefully before we try to readjust
them. Some are cheerfully adaptable to systems and organizations; others resist every effort to make them conform,
and find even honors programs, advanced placement courses,
and the like, distasteful because they involve submission to
what someone else thinks is good for them. When we think
of talented students, we are thinking of future intellectual
leaders, and it will never do to forget that the child who is
a joy in the classroom and the brightest ornament of the
Honors Convocation may be less likely to change the
world's ways of thought than the little devil who failed
every subject but the one he liked to study, who stubbornly
refused to "go out for" anything, and who throughout his
school years remained a disagreeable prig. Too great precision in definition and too much insistence on preconceived
programs can result in the selection of the clever and the
quick rather than the truly intelligent and original.[7]

In the end, the academically talented student is the one

whom the experienced and sympathetic teacher, using all information available to him—test scores, grades, interviews, etc.—declares to be such; the more immediate and personal the judgment can be, the less likelihood there is of serious error. In the matter of students as individualistic, infinitely varied, and—one might add—socially valuable as these, mechanical definitions and mass procedures are at best unreliable and at worst unjust. To find the bright boys and girls is relatively easy; as Terman pointed out years ago, they are at the top in virtually everything, and any skimming operation, wisely and kindly administered, will bring them in. And let there be no misunderstanding: these are fine young people, potentially very valuable citizens, for whom any democratic school system is bound to do everything it can. But if we want our schools to devote any large share of their energies to the training of intellectual leaders, we shall have to learn to look for them not only among the happy, well-adjusted, efficient youngsters who win all the honors, but also among the dirty and unkempt, the socially unacceptable, the wild and obstreperous, the one-track minds, and even the scholastic failures.[8] For these, there is no substitute for the sympathetic understanding that comes only from long experience in dealing with children—the understanding that can pierce through surface appearances to distinguish worth from worthlessness, that knows instinctively when to bend the rules and when to apply them with steely rigidity, and that never permits humanitarianism to degenerate into sentimentality. If there is any one criticism that I should be inclined to make of the schools, it is that they are too hesitant to trust human understanding, whether in the selection of superior students or in any other matter, and prefer to use tests and statistics, apparently under the conviction that such "objective" and "scientific" methods will serve them more reliably. They are easier to administer, and decisions based on them easier to defend: cold figures deposited by infallible calculating machines admit of no argument. They undoubtedly make few mistakes in selecting the bright boys and girls; they also collect along with them the slick grade-getters and expert test-passers. What we do not know is how many original and creative minds they pass by. It needs to be said, in conclusion, that the kind of human understanding that might spot the incipient genius is less common in the schools than we might like: the guidance officer, on whom such chores usually fall, is more likely to have gained his post by earning hours of credit than by demonstrating any special gift for sizing up the adolescent mind. Some of these guidance officers, to be sure, are splendid; nearly all of them are sincere and conscientious. Their weaknesses are those of all specialists, who inevitably see problems in terms of their own specialties. But my greatest objection to most of them is a very simple one: they are too young. Time might remedy this if they did not tend, as they grow older, to slip out of guidance and into administration. Conant's insistence on a certain numerical ratio between guidance counselors and students as a requisite for the effective high school (*The American High School Today*, pp. 44–45) seems to me to miss the point. Half as many wise old heads, long battered against intransigent adolescents (especially if some of these were their own children), would be more helpful. Perhaps, at that, we are safer with the machines.

Assuming that we can satisfactorily select our roster of academically talented students, the next question is what to do with them. At the risk of putting the academic cart before the horse, I should like to begin by suggesting a number of things that possibly had better *not* be done. The first of these is the speed-up, the high-pressure process, that puts the talented student through the old, familiar course of study at double or triple the usual rate, never considering whether the course itself might be in need of revision or whether the constant pressure on the student to "keep up" really enables him to learn faster or just leaves him breathless and harried.[9] Mathematicians say that mathematics classes for the gifted all too often do little more than cover obsolete topics at a high rate of speed. Such a process in any subject seems singularly unprofitable. A history class that merely force-feeds in one semester the same dull, badly written book that is normally spread over two, may keep the student hopping but is scarcely calculated either to teach him more history or to awaken and sustain his interest in the subject. The worst feature of the speed-up process is that it turns intellectual disciplines into academic steeplechases, complete with water traps in the form of the coveted "good grades." It tends to focus the student's attention on his record rather than on learning; at its worst, it leads to the deliberate calculation of how much he must learn in order to earn this or that grade, and the budgeting of his time and energy accordingly. While it is undoubtedly true that the superior student in our schools has much too easy a time of it [10] and that the tempo of his study could be stepped up considerably without doing him any harm, it is also true that mere bearing down has no intrinsic value, educational or moral, and may in fact be destructive of the very qualities we most want. The experience of the war years showed us that speed and pressure, especially when accompanied by strict discipline and strong motivation, can turn the talented young man into a technical expert with efficiency and dispatch; whether it can also make an educated man of him remains an open question.[11]

Another device for the education of the talented against which I feel bound to sound a note of caution is the class—or "seminar," as it is more commonly styled—in critical thinking. This is a concept much beloved of contemporary educators; that the school must "teach students to think" has become an Article of Faith, and one disagrees with it at his peril.[12] How often did I hear teachers and administrators say, as if with a sense of shame and failure, that their students "had done nothing but learn facts!" It is almost as if the acquisition of factual knowledge, like certain bodily functions, were not quite presentable and should be carried on only behind a veil of furious mental activity. Merely to equip a talented youngster with a store of information is regarded as a dereliction of duty; "rote learning must be replaced by thought learning." [13]

It is undoubtedly true that facts learned in a context of relationships, so that not only the fact but its position in a system are known, are absorbed more pleasantly and make a longer-lasting impression on the mind than do facts merely memorized. In so far as there is time enough for it, this is the method to be preferred, and every competent teacher will use it just as much as he can. Unfortunately, it is more time-consuming than simple memorization, and in a world so full of things to learn, the rote list can never be entirely dispensed with. Facts *must* be learned, and however much our teachers might wish it were not so, we may rest assured that they know it *is* so and that they act accordingly.

For the bright student, memorization seems particularly inappropriate. He learns quickly; he absorbs and stores away at a glance what his slower contemporaries may pore over for hours without much effect. His mind is lively and demanding; he loves taking ideas apart and putting them together again; he grasps relationships quickly; he can generalize from particulars. His great need seems to be for some kind of mental discipline, something to make him do all these things critically, i.e., with a proper regard for logic and a proper sensitivity to consequences. He cannot be left to ride off madly in all directions at once.

The sensible answer to this would certainly seem to be some kind of training in critical thinking, and at first glance it may seem strange that anyone should feel uncomfortable about it. The trouble is that many school people insist on acting as if critical thinking were a subject and not a process, as if it were something that could be studied and mastered by and for itself, quite without regard to the subject matter over which it was being exercised. I do not mean that they attempt to teach it in the abstract: this would bring them to logic and mathematics, which would be perfectly sound. Rather, they try to train the student to think critically about bodies of information with which he has only the sketchiest acquaintance, where he does not know and at his stage of education cannot possibly know enough to check the validity of his premises and the soundness of his conclusions.

This kind of course has two serious faults. The first of these is carelessness about matters of fact. While it is true that high school youngsters cannot be expected to have a professional expert's command of facts, it is vitally important that the facts they do have be accurate and that discussion of these facts—critical thinking about them—be kept within the limits of the factual knowledge actually possessed by the class. This can be done and has been done for untold ages by skillful teachers; in fact, it is my observation that critical thinking in this sense is a part of every good teacher's method. But it is used only after the class has mastered the body of fact over which it is to be exercised: they have studied the chapter or read the play or story or whatnot and are familiar with its factual content; now they begin a critical analysis of this body of fact, studying the relation of its parts, looking for flaws in reasoning, putting ideas together to draw inferences of their own, relating what they have learned here to what they have learned somewhere else, and so on. And as the discussion proceeds, the teacher has an ear out for the slightest error of fact or for attempts to launch into speculation and guesswork that will take the class outside the limits of what they know.

By contrast, the class in critical thinking commonly distinguishes itself by a cavalier disregard for factual information. It usually consists of a miscellaneous group of students, often simply the top 1 per cent or some such figure of the student body, who rarely have any extensive common store of information. Each student is encouraged to pursue his own interest and to make reports on it to the class, which then proceeds to "critically think" about the material thus presented to them. One student may report on radioactive isotopes, another on a story by William Faulkner, another on race relations; the theory seems to be that all should feel free to discuss all or any of these topics, whether or not they know anything about them and regardless of where the discussion may lead.

I recall several examples of this sort of thing. In one case a student reported on the English Reformation; the report was good, showed careful study and sound reasoning. At its conclusion the teacher called for discussion. Since nobody else in the class—including, I fear, the teacher—knew much about the English Reformation, the subsequent interplay of questions and answers was something less than illuminating. Finally some enterprising youngster thought of John Calvin and raised the question of his influence on the English church. Not to make a long story of it, the class ended up discussing predestination and total depravity, about which nobody—this time including both the teacher and the student who made the report—knew anything whatsoever. They attempted to apply these doctrines, which they did not understand at all, to moral standards in our country today, about which they knew no more than do most teen-age youngsters. The discussion was lively; many of the students showed keen wit and quick perception. Interest never flagged, and half-truths flew back and forth at a terrific rate.

In another case the class had read an essay on friendship. As long as the discussion confined itself to the essay and to other works that the students knew, it was eminently worth while, but it soon got out of hand and ended in a lively and quite uninformative—because uninformed—debate as to whether boys or girls get "madder" at each other when friendships between them end. In still another instance an article in a popular magazine occasioned a lively and uninformative discussion of local race relations, in which fact was replaced by newspaper gossip and hearsay, and principle by pious platitude. The point is that in each instance the school had forgotten the basic principle of all critical thinking: that *knowledge must precede criticism*. The teacher is forever responsible to the fact; when he disregards that responsibility, he makes a travesty of the art of teaching, no matter how keen the interest and how great the delight of his class. Too often the exercise in critical thinking is permitted to pull loose from its anchor in fact and to become a bright and sparkling little game in which the prize goes to the quick-witted rather than to the thoughtful. When this happens, we have confused conversation, the purpose of which is entertainment, with education, the purpose of which is learning. As a device for lightening a dull day or spicing up a class session gone stale and unprofitable, conversation is entirely appropriate; it may even have solid worth as a motivational device. But it bears only the most superficial resemblance to critical thinking.

This brings me to my second objection to classes or "seminars" of this kind, and that is that they are all too likely to give the student a false impression of the nature of the learning process. He is led to think of it as a delightful and rather exciting social diversion in which one picks up information effortlessly and allows the mind to leap and soar over the general applications and implications of a subject. Dull fundamentals are laid aside or given a quick once-over; masses of detail—those tiresome lists of names and processes and formulas and categories—are left to the professional and his plodding apprentices. True education—and what other kind does the gifted student want?—consists of "broadening the understandings and deepening the insights," and for this what could be better than the impounded coruscations of a group of high-voltage intellects, flashing back and forth in an atmosphere of good fellowship? This is fun; it is also excellent social training of a kind American culture could use to advantage, for as conversationalists we are a dull people. But it is not learning, and we do wrong when we lead our students to think it is. Learning is not a social activity; it is a lonely business, and it produces loneliness—the greater the learning, the greater the loneliness. It is not fun, though it has its moments of joy and exhilaration; it is hard, tedious work, often exasperating and commonly discouraging. It is full of repetition, of dull fact-gathering, of monotonous checking and rechecking of details. It demands discipline—forcing the mind to do what it does not want to do. It requires endless memorization, for the learner will never have time for the final step to understanding if he must be forever running to his reference books. We have no right, as teachers, to let our students— and above all, our best students—imagine that learning is or can be anything else than all of this. Young people, especially highly intelligent young people, are by nature impatient; the course in critical thinking with its air of ease and speed, with its promise of an educational reward greater than that to be gained from "doing nothing but learning facts," is a questionable service to them and to society.

Do I mean to suggest by all this that I am opposed to critical thinking or to teaching students to think? Of course not. Critical thinking is an important educational discipline, and probably close to the oldest of them all. Nobody ever really knows anything until he has made a critical analysis of it and carefully surveyed its implications and consequences. Ordinarily, like most intellectual activities, critical thinking is a solitary process; it is profitable as a group activity only if all in the group are thoroughly familiar with the subject under discussion, so that all are operating from a common factual base. This is hardly more than normal classroom procedure; I have seen it in so many classes, elementary, secondary, and college, that I wonder why anyone should have imagined that it was *not* going on. As for "teaching students to think," I suspect that the correct word is "allowing" rather than "teaching" and that in using the phrase we are seeking to avoid two educational evils: (1) doing the student's thinking for him, i.e., making so complete an exposition that nothing is left for the student to do but to absorb, and (2) cramming the course with so much factual material that the student has no time to sort it out. In this sense, no teacher in his right mind would be opposed to "teaching students to think." But when the phrase is used to defend idle chitchat and the exchange of shallow, ill-informed opinions *in place of* the acquisition and careful study of facts, then, in company with most of my colleagues, I shudder.

Both in the literature and in the schools there is much discussion of acceleration and enrichment as devices for improving the quality of education for the superior student. Unfortunately, as in the case of so many other pedagogical terms, it is hard to find a clear definition of either of the two, let alone one with which all teachers would agree. To some, acceleration means "skipping," to others it means no more than the speed-up. Still others think of it as releasing the student from the twin lock steps of chronology and the formal course and permitting him to move ahead at the speed that is appropriate to him. To others it means allowing the able student to carry more than the normal load of courses, thus completing the requirements for graduation in less than the usual time. Some think of it in terms of early admission to the educational process—to kindergarten or first grade; others think of early admission to college and of the various devices by which this may be effected.[14]

It is obvious that, however worded, described, or implemented, acceleration always contemplates a quickening of the educational pace, and its basic aim is to put the student through more educational experiences faster. It may result either in getting him to his ultimate educational goal sooner or in augmenting the number of experiences that he may have within a given period of time, or in both. Its basic premise is that the talented student learns at a higher rate of speed than his ordinary fellows and that one good way to provide him with a program of study suited to his needs is to take advantage of this fact. As he masters one phase of a subject, he is enabled to move on to the next without having to wait while the slower students catch up to him and without having to spend time on repetitive drill that for him is unnecessary. Depending on how the work is organized, he can do this because he is released from class routine and allowed to work on his own, or because the class itself is organized in the "ungraded" fashion, or because he has been assigned to an ability group in which all members are moving at an accelerated pace. The first scheme is frequently an improvisation devised to meet an immediate need. The second is more common in the elementary than in the secondary schools; probably the best-known example is the much-publicized one of the San Angelo, Texas, schools. It was used, reportedly with great success, at Monroe High School, Rochester, N.Y., for some years, where it was abandoned chiefly because the numbers grew too great. The accelerated group is, of course, the result of the practice of segregating students according to ability; this will be discussed later. The immediate advantage to the student is that his education proceeds at the rate that is natural to him; his interest is maintained by a flow of new topics and problems coming at a rate that is satisfactory to him. Furthermore, he is spared the tedium of mere timeserving; he does not lose interest through boredom nor run the risk of developing lazy ways and bad study habits, as the bright student is all too likely to do if the work is too easy.[15] From the long-range point of view he is enabled to cut at least some time off an educational experience that is becoming unconscionably long for all who have scholarly or professional ambitions. The saving of as little as six months can mean a great deal professionally, financially, and personally; it has real meaning, too, in terms of service rendered to society.

The disadvantages of acceleration are partly educational, partly social. It may degenerate into a high-pressure program that leaves the talented youngster no time for thought and maturation; it may become a mere speed-up, unintelligently force-feeding stale and uninspired materials. Of these evils I have already spoken. One danger not so often noted in the literature but almost always mentioned by teachers lies in the fact that in judging when the student may be allowed to move ahead, mastery may be too quickly assumed. Momentary comprehension is rarely enough for sound learning; points need not only to be understood but to be nailed down, so to speak, by some repetitive drill, even for the talented student. This is certainly true in such cumulative subjects as mathematics and foreign languages; in the latter, particularly, a great deal of repetition is required if anything resembling mastery is to be attained. In complex subjects like English and history, it is difficult to tell when the student has learned and understood enough so that he may safely move on; superficiality is a constant danger. No matter what accelerative scheme is used, it is of the greatest importance that the work be not permitted to degenerate into wave-top skittering. In the accelerated course, as in all others, we are looking for sound learning commensurate with the student's age and educational experience; acceleration is pedagogically valid only so long as it remains consonant with that aim.

As for the social aspect of acceleration, this looms rather less large than it might have a few years ago. There is still some concern among educators for fear it may throw a student's emotional and social development out of gear; he may not be able to adapt himself without undue strain to a group in which he is younger, physically less developed, and socially less experienced than the rest, and the problems thus created may outweigh the educational advantages. Obviously if he is placed in an ability group consisting of others like himself, the social problem is solved for the moment, but if through acceleration he graduates from high school earlier than usual, it arises again. The feeling is widespread among teachers that there is an enormous gulf between the ages of 17 and 18—the age at which the student normally passes from high school to college—and they view with misgivings schemes that would permit the 15- or 16-year-old to leave the relatively protected and regimented domain of the high school for the somewhat heady independence of the college campus. He may not be ready for so much freedom; in addition, he may find himself brushed aside by his older classmates as too young and inexperienced to share their social activities. He may end by becoming a recluse—that worst of all fates in the eyes of a socially minded educator—or run into serious emotional maladjustment. However, there are clear signs that this particular objection to acceleration is losing ground; experience has not borne out our fears as often or in as serious degree as we thought: high school youngsters admitted to college classes have in general done well in their studies and suffered no serious dislocation of their social life.[16] And a revived and most refreshing interest in the individual and his intellectual development is making decided inroads on a philosophy of education that had made a shibboleth of social adjustment. In general, it may be asserted with some confidence that acceleration, in one form or another, and to one degree or another, has become an accepted part of most programs for the academically talented in the elementary and secondary schools. Probably the chief question as yet unanswered is whether the accelerated student is best left in his own school and age group, and the appropriate advanced work brought down the educational ladder to him (as in the Advanced Placement Program), or whether he had better be moved up the ladder to the work for which he is ready (as in "skipping" or "early admission"). Perhaps we can best hope that current concern for the individual will cause that question to be answered not in terms of the mass but in terms of *this* student and *that* student, with the work being brought down to the student or the student moved up to the work as shall seem best and wisest in each individual case.

Acceleration, for all that it may be applied in different ways and differently defined in accord with the way in which it is applied, has in all instances the basic characteristic of increased speed: it always means that in some way the pace of learning is being stepped up. Among the definitions of enrichment, it is much harder to find even that much common ground; the degree of confusion is well indicated by the fact that it is variously described as a "plan," a "policy," and a "technique," that it is sometimes viewed as an entity distinct from acceleration and ability grouping and sometimes as a supercategory that includes them both.[17] Perhaps our best course will be to think of enrichment as a response to the fact that the talented student learns more things, just as acceleration is a response to learning them faster. And to prevent any overlap—for obviously the student who learns faster may also learn more, and vice versa— let us think of any subject as having a central core consisting of those fundamental parts without a mastery of which no one can be said to know it at all. This central core is, of course, not static; it grows with the age and experience of the student. The experienced and skillful teacher at each educational level can define it, for it is the factual base on which he organizes his teaching. Acceleration means that the student is set to mastering this core of essentials at a rate of efficiency and speed higher than the ordinary. Besides this core, the subject also has ramifications and amplifications, relations with other subjects, and so on—some more, some less significant, but all contributing to its totality. Enrichment means that the study of a judicious selection of these is added to mastery of the core.[18]

Like acceleration, enrichment is an old pedagogical device, long used by teachers to help bright youngsters explore aspects of a subject for which the duller cannot afford the time. In its simplest form it consists of little more than extra assignments (e.g., to read two plays of Shakespeare while the rest of the class reads one) or collateral reading (e.g., to read Franklin's *Autobiography* in addition to regularly assigned readings on the period of the American Revolution).[19] A somewhat more elaborate form is the "project" or "research problem," in which the student is set to investigating parts of the subject for which the regular class has no time, and which require supplementary study and investigation, often to be carried on with little help from the teacher. Sometimes a whole class of talented students will be set to doing this kind of study, each individual pursuing a problem of his own choosing, with the various problems having no more immediate relation to each other than that they are all concerned with one general subject, e.g., science. From here on, enrichment may be made as elaborate as desired; it may include trips to strategic spots (factories, the public library, city council or school board meetings, court sessions, points of historical interest, etc.), talks by local experts and professional men and women (this is called "utilization of community resources"), attendance at plays, concerts, and so on.[20] A particularly effective type of enrichment is embodied in the summer school institute, in which selected students are given several weeks of uninterrupted study of a subject of their choice, with all the school's facilities at their disposal and under the direction of specially chosen teachers.[21] Still another type consists of the after-hours or Saturday class, in which students are led by a teacher or local expert in the study of specialized or advanced topics in some field of interest, e.g., in higher mathematics. The list of possible variations is virtually limitless; it might well end with a reference to Cleveland's major work classes, which are full-time projects involving the enrichment technique.[22]

The advantages of enrichment, as opposed to acceleration, are numerous. In the first place, it does not displace the student from his normal age group; no "skipping" or other such dislocation is involved; instead, the student progresses through the series of grades in the regular order and in the canonical number of years. Moving along in this way in the company of his peers, he is faced with few unusual social and emotional problems; he never has to bear the dubious distinction of being the chubby genius. At the same time he is enabled to study more intensively, to follow out in greater breadth and depth, those subjects for which he has shown special aptitude. In the end, although he will earn his diploma no sooner than the others and presumably have no more credits than they, the content of his education will be literally "enriched"; he will have acquired knowledge and skills more nearly commensurate with his capabilities. His fund of educational experiences, both in breadth and depth, will be larger than the ordinary, and he will to that degree be better prepared to proceed to college work.

One aspect of enrichment that receives relatively little attention is motivation; setting the student to work on some specialty or side issue that interests him may illuminate the whole subject for him and show him values that had never occurred to him before. I recall the case of a student in an English class who had shown no interest in the subject at all until, in a supplementary reading list, he hit on *Huckle-*

berry Finn. From there, he went right down the list of Mark Twain's books, reading every one he could get hold of. On the day of my visit he was giving a report on *Life on the Mississippi*. I doubt if he will ever find English tedious again, for Twain opened the subject up for him. Such experiences are not unique or rare, as any teacher knows; to trigger them is one of the things that makes teaching worth-while.

In addition, the enrichment program can offer unusual opportunity for original and creative work, quite without detracting from the attention that must be given to fundamentals. It can be, and usually is, free of high pressure and the speed-up; if it is properly organized, the student takes on only as much in the way of enriched study as he can afford. It allows for the development of the individual, for self-expression, since all do not have to do the same things or work in the same way or at the same pace. In actual fact, the enrichment program, if directed wisely and humanely, simply makes educational capital of the natural tendency of the highly intelligent youngster to explore his environment, to read, to observe, to investigate, and to experiment.

On the debit side, it is of course obvious that enrichment saves no time; it may bring the student to the end of his educational path better trained and more knowledgeable, but it will not bring him there sooner. As I remarked earlier, saving of time can be of great value, both to the individual himself and to society; furthermore, for the truly able and intelligent person, education does not end with schooling but is a lifetime activity. In view of this fact, the extra education gained by enrichment may not be as valuable as the time saved by acceleration. The talented individual is going to go on learning anyway, and it matters not at all whether he does his learning before or after he completes his formal education. On this particular point, the scale of values is very delicately poised indeed.

Rather more serious is the danger that enrichment may degenerate into pseudointellectual play, with more emphasis on pleasure and enthusiasm than on learning. Measuring the height of the local radio tower may be legitimate enrichment for the mathematics class, but one may question the value of a study of Mendelssohn's *Midsummer Night's Dream* music for the understanding of Shakespeare's play.[23] The same may be said for all purely illustrative projects, such as painting posters, making sketches and models, soap-carving, doll-dressing, and the like. All these devices, and many others like them, constitute little more than incidental activity, some of which may be educative and some not. Its proper role in education is like that of conversation: a device to lighten a dull day. It is fun; it often has motivational value, but it bears about the same relation to genuine enrichment that conversation does to critical thinking.

In any program of enrichment there is always the danger that students may be introduced prematurely to aspects of a subject that depend for their proper understanding on a thorough mastery of fundamentals. To set a group of high school youngsters, for example, to conducting a survey of public opinion, even on some relatively trivial subject, has grave educational dangers, the least of which is the misinformation that will undoubtedly be collected. No high school student, and, I suspect, not too many high school teachers, has any idea of the complexity and delicacy of such a sociological operation, of the subtle way in which questions must be phrased, the complex process involved in the selection of persons to be interviewed, the proper establishment of controls, and the weighing and balancing of replies. Opinion surveying is for the trained and experienced professional; to permit high school youngsters to attempt it is to run the grave risk of misleading them about the nature of the subject they are studying, to oversimplify the learning process, and to leave them with the delightful and deadly feeling that it's all very smooth sailing and great sport. The same danger lies in every type of enrichment project, even down to the use of the term "research" in describing it. For if it is true research, it is likely to be premature; if it is not true research, it is almost certain to mislead the student as to what research really is. Talented and imaginative young people have an almost fatal facility for seeing how a problem is bound to be answered; set them somewhere near the end of the problem and they will work out the final steps with great joy and dispatch. But ask them to start at the beginning and—like the genuine scholar or scientist—work out the *whole* solution, step by step, and they are quickly bored. The former they do with ease; the latter they must be compelled to do. Enrichment is valid as an educational technique only so long as it compels intellectual discipline, and, so to speak, keeps its eye on the educational ball, which is progressive mastery of central subject matter; lacking careful control, it is as likely to descend to wave-top skittering as is acceleration—and the fact that the skittering is done off-course instead of on-course is no great advantage. Enrichment cannot be justified solely as "study in breadth." [24]

Whether the program for the talented student is to take the form of enrichment, acceleration, or both, the next question is whether it is to be accompanied by ability grouping. This comes close to being an explosive subject in educational circles; feelings for and against grouping are likely to run quite high. In general, and at the risk of oversimplifying the case, one may say that working teachers by and large tend to favor ability grouping, with fairly strong support from parents and administrators.[25] Most college teachers are firmly, not to say vociferously, on the side of grouping, and there is some evidence that their students tend to agree with them.[26] Disagreement and scepticism seem to come largely from the educational theorists and from those educators to whom the social aspect of education remains paramount. The theorists are concerned for fear ability grouping may be undertaken before it has been clearly defined and categorized, before all its aspects have been investigated and objective criteria established for the selection of different kinds of groups. Many of them, too, are still unconvinced that ability grouping is a significant factor in increasing or improving learning; they point to many other elements in the learning situation that to their way of thinking are as critical as ability.[27] For the "social adjustment" educator, the dangers of emotional and social maladjustment, particularly those associated with the idea of an elite, make grouping a questionable practice.[28]

The fact is, of course, that all high schools practice some kind of ability grouping and have done so for years. Rare indeed is the school that does not distinguish between college preparatory students and others; even if the college preparatory classes are open to all students, their lessons are designed with college in mind, and students not intending to go to college will tend to pass them by. Some subjects, too, have a way of being, so to speak, self-grouping. Mathematics and the languages tend to enroll those who have an aptitude for them and to exclude those who do not, whether or not the school makes a deliberate attempt to bring this about; the same may be said for physics, and, to a lesser degree, for chemistry. Grouping may sometimes occur through the merest accident: all the best students may just happen to elect the same class. The real question is not whether there is to be grouping, but whether grouping shall be carried on systematically, according to a predetermined plan, and what that plan shall be.

For our present purpose, we can dismiss all grouping not based on academic ability (i.e., ability to pursue the standard, old-line, college preparatory subjects). In so doing, we are relying largely on some basic pedagogical facts, borne out by the experience of many teachers: first, that some students do learn these subjects more readily and easily than others; second, that we can—at least for all practical purposes—sort out the abler from the less able in this respect; and, finally, that the resultant groups can be taught more efficiently and effectively than can undifferentiated groups. Homogeneity, from the point of view of the educational psychologist, may be more of a pious hope than an actuality; [29] it may well be that the abilities of a homogeneous group will scatter all up and down the scale within a few weeks after the group has been constituted; it may be true that, in the top group, the range of ability will be very wide —from, say, IQ 130 to IQ 180, or even higher—and that the difference between IQ 180 and IQ 130 is as spectacular as that between IQ 130 and IQ 80; the fact remains that the "homogeneous" group—for that is its accepted name—is easier for the teacher to handle, learns more readily, works together better, and creates fewer discipline or personality problems than does the unselected class, and that this is true not just of the top group but of all groups, including even the lowest and slowest. The theory that the slower groups will lose their spirit if they are deprived of the stimulation supplied by the abler students seems not to be borne out by experience. On the contrary, not only do the able students find the slower ones a drag on their enthusiasm and a sore trial to their patience, but the slower find the bright a constant irritation and a bitterly discouraging reminder, thrust before their faces day after day, of what they themselves are unable to accomplish.[30] Students grouped homogeneously will find a level of learning on which they can all operate with relative ease and a minimum of friction; at this level they sort themselves out into those who lead and those who follow, but the distance and the differences between the two are not great enough to create invidious distinctions or feelings of jealousy or of impatience. Operating at a speed comfortable for them all, and with sets of ideas that they all find within their grasp, they stimulate each other horizontally, so to speak, in a way far more effective than any vertical stimulation, from bright to slow, could provide. Grouping implies, of course, not merely a difference in pace but a difference in course content and course goals. To set all groups to covering the same materials, but simply at different rates of speed, is a travesty of ability grouping. I wish all those who doubt the effectiveness of grouping could have the experience I had of visiting on one day all five levels of a single course, all of them, as it happened, discussing the same topic. Each treated it in the way proper to the group; the learning in each group was on the level appropriate to its membership. There was virtually 100 per cent participation in every group; no one stole the limelight; no one hung back for fear of making himself look foolish. The discussion of the top group would have done honor to any college class; that of the lowest hardly rose above the simplest observations; everyone in every group learned something that meant something *to him*. That this was in part due to expert teaching I cheerfully admit, but it should be remembered that in a homogeneous group the teacher can use his *ex-*

pertise on *teaching* and not on trying to keep an ill-assorted roomful of lively adolescents from falling apart. The lesson of experience is that ability grouping, if practiced with wisdom, good sense, and a due regard for human feelings, is beneficial to all groups, the lowest as well as the highest. There is more learning and better learning at every level; there is greater satisfaction to the student; teaching is more effective; and the groups seem to minimize social distinctions rather than to accentuate them.[31]

In general, there are two types of ability grouping in the schools: (1) grouping across the board (by "rail" or "track"), and (2) grouping by subject. The "track" or "rail" system normally provides that the student shall take *all* his classes on the level to which his ability has assigned him. It is practiced only in large high schools where the number of students is large enough to ensure full class enrollments at every level.[32] Much more common is grouping by subject. This has many manifest advantages, the first and most obvious being the fact that it recognizes the diversity of human gifts: few are gifted in all subjects, or even in all those called academic; a realistic plan for grouping ought to take due account of this. When grouping is done by subject, a student may qualify for the top group in, say, English, but find himself in an average group in foreign language and perhaps even in a slow group in mathematics.[33] The greatest single difficulty in grouping by subject is a mechanical but nonetheless vexing one: scheduling. Shuffling class schedules in such a way as to make sure that an appropriate ability group in the appropriate subject will be available to each student constitutes a major challenge to the administrator; the effectiveness of grouping can be seriously damaged or even completely nullified if, through the exigencies of scheduling, nonqualified students are permitted to slip into high-level groups. My observations of the schools suggest that this is a danger far more common than its opposite, i.e., the inability of the *qualified* student to fit an appropriate ability group into his schedule. More than one teacher reported to me, somewhat unhappily, that his carefully organized "honors" class had been torpedoed by the assignment to it of unqualified students "who couldn't take the subject at any other hour." The real and basic difficulty here is the crippling rule regarding class size, under which practically every school labors: the administrator must not only watch his hours of meeting, but he must also remember that he may not permit the enrollment in any class to fall below the minimum prescribed by the school board.

Grouping by subject is rarely to be found outside fairly sizeable schools, i.e., those with a total enrollment of four hundred or more. It does not require quite so large a student body as does the "track" system, since in any given group of students there will be more who qualify for high-level groups in one or two subjects than in all. Moreover, grouping by subject is rather more flexible and adaptable to immediate circumstances and needs than is "track" grouping; groups in one or another subject can be instituted or dropped according to demand; the number of groups within a given subject is similarly variable.

As to whether membership in groups should be mandatory or voluntary, the practice of the schools is varied. Some feel that the student should be informed of his eligibility for this or that group, and then left free to decide whether or not to join it. This plan is the usual one where grouping is limited to "regular" and "honors" sections or to a "general" and a "college preparatory" course.[34] Where grouping is more elaborate, as in the larger schools, it is frequently mandatory; the student is required to join the ability group for which he is declared eligible, and may withdraw from it only by permission of the appropriate school official.[35] It seems fair to say that as long as grouping consists chiefly or entirely of siphoning off the one or two highest ability groups into honors courses of one kind or another, membership in the groups may well be voluntary; the decision to be made is a relatively simple one—whether or not to engage in a more demanding program of study—and there is real merit in giving the student the satisfaction of making the choice himself. But when grouping involves all levels, from the highest to the lowest, it is hardly possible to inform the student of his qualifications and let him choose which group he will enter: a few wrong choices would throw the whole system into confusion. It is, of course, to be assumed that the student's choice, in any case, is limited to the decision to join or not to join a group *for which he has been declared eligible.* If he is free to choose a group above that level, then there is no ability grouping in any real sense of the word. In any event, whether grouping be voluntary or mandatory, it is essential that a proper mechanism be provided for shifting students from one group to another so that the "late bloomer" may have a chance to get into his proper group as soon as he is ready to do so, and so that errors in the original selection may be corrected with as little grief as possible.

As for the number of ability groups that should be set up, this is partly an educational and partly an administrative problem. Laying aside the question of "track" grouping versus "subject" grouping and leaving out of consideration grouping that consists of segregation at the top level alone, into how many ability groups are we to divide our students? Here again there is great variety in the schools. The largest high schools distinguish as many as five levels in academic subjects; [36] for schools of modest enrollment so large a number is rarely feasible, and in many instances may not even be advisable. A sensible and practical scheme, and one that is being more and more widely considered, is the "20-60-20" plan. It is based on the theory that the groups likely to gain the most from homogeneity are the highest and the lowest; accordingly, the top 20 per cent and the lowest 20 per cent are drawn off into segregated groups, and the middle 60 per cent are left undifferentiated. This is a little hard on the middle group, which is in effect denied the advantages of both heterogeneity and homogeneity; they are also rather likely, in the nature of things, to be assigned to the less able teachers, since the best teachers may well be drawn off for the benefit of the top group and to cope with the special problems posed by the lowest. Probably we must hope that as ability grouping establishes its educational worth, it will be extended to the middle 60 per cent; in the meantime we can justify the special opportunity given to the top 20 per cent on grounds that the education of the gifted has been too long neglected and has fair claim for the moment to a little extra consideration. Special help for slow students has been so long an accepted part of our educational system that the segregation of the lowest 20 per cent needs no defense at this point. The real danger in the 20-60-20 plan resides in the fact that the top group may be too large and cover too wide a range of ability; if its "floor" falls much below the level indicated by IQ 120, it will lose much of its claim to homogeneity and its attendant advantages. In fact, I should go so far as to venture the opinion that unless the top group is so constituted as to gather within itself only the very ablest students in the school, it will be hard to justify its existence; ability grouping that does not have as its first and major purpose the real improvement of educational opportunity for the academically talented student is hardly more than an expensive pedagogical experiment and had better be left for that dreamed-of day when the schools have all the money they need and can do all the experimenting they like.

II

THE ADVANCED
PLACEMENT
PROGRAM

Among the many schemes and programs that have been devised for enriching and accelerating the education of academically talented students, the Advanced Placement Program stands out as not only sound and sensible but also as having very wide applicability. There are few schools, public or independent, large or small, urban or rural, that could not institute Advanced Placement in one form or another and in at least one subject; for the student the Program offers both immediate, practical rewards and long-range educational advantages. In continuous operation since the fall of 1953, the Program has passed its probationary stage and deserves to be regarded as an established institution. Few faults, if any, have been found in it by students, teachers, or administrators, whether on the secondary or college level; praise and satisfaction have been well-nigh universal.[1]

Briefly, the Advanced Placement Program affords the exceptionally able high school student the opportunity of pursuing courses of college level in his high school and under his high school teachers. Courses are provided in eleven subjects: English, mathematics, French, German, Spanish, Latin, American history, European history, biology, chemistry, and physics. These, it should be noticed, are the sub-

jects most immediately germane to college work; they are in the direct stream of educational progress; they are the foundations on which the traditional liberal arts program of the American college is based. None is merely peripheral; none, at this stage of education, may be considered over-specialized. Upon a judicious selection among them and the careful, thorough study of those selected, success in college depends.[2]

The original impetus to the Program was given by President Gordon Chalmers, of Kenyon College, and Dr. William Cornog, then principal of Philadelphia Central High School, now superintendent of New Trier High School, Winnetka, Illinois. That it began as the joint effort of a college and a high school man has proved significant of its development at every stage and of its present state; it is, has always been, and hopefully will always be a co-operative enterprise, resting upon the combined efforts of both secondary schools and colleges, directed and implemented by high school and college teachers of the various subjects, working together. Financed during its first two years by a grant from the Fund for the Advancement of Education, it was subsequently taken over by the College Entrance Examination Board, which now administers it with the assistance and co-operation of the Educational Testing Service of Princeton, N.J.

The basic intent of the Program is twofold: first, to provide the academically talented student with a deeper and broader educational experience in the high school than he might ordinarily obtain, thus preparing him more effectively for college work; and second, to enable him to earn college credit while he is still in high school and thus to accelerate his progress toward his final educational objective, whatever that may be. The actual granting of college credit for Advanced Placement courses must of course remain the prerogative of the colleges; nonetheless, the policies of the better colleges and universities have been quite liberal in this respect from the beginning, and the disposition to allow credit toward the bachelor's degree for Advanced Placement courses successfully completed is spreading rapidly among collegiate institutions all over the country.

The plan of the Advanced Placement Program could hardly be clearer or simpler. There is no organization that must be joined by the school or the college; there are no dues to be paid or formal commitments to be made; the Program itself lays down no requirements as to selection of teachers or students, and prescribes nothing with respect to the organization, scheduling, or conduct of the courses. Any school that desires to give Advanced Placement work is free to do so at any time and in any manner that it chooses, with or without prior contact with the administrative offices of the Program.[3] Assistance and advice from these offices are always available, but there are no prescriptive rules and regulations.

At only one point are there any formalities to be observed. Each year, in May, the Program administers national examinations in each of the eleven subjects covered by Advanced Placement, and these must be taken by the students if they wish to present, to the collegiate institution of their choice, a request for credit toward the bachelor's degree for the work they have pursued. These examinations are prepared each year by a committee of high school and college teachers of the subject in question, who are appointed by the College Entrance Examination Board and who work together in formulating the questions. The examinations are designed to occupy three hours and are almost entirely of the essay type, although some are supplemented by objective tests and, in the case of the modern foreign languages, by tapes designed to test oral comprehension. These examinations are as follows: English literature and composition, mathematics (analytic geometry and calculus), biology, chemistry, physics, American history, European history, French 4, German 3, German 4, Spanish 4, Latin 4, and Latin 5.[4] In the fall of each year the school is asked to notify the College Entrance Examination Board of the number of its students who may be expected to take the examinations in each subject in the following spring.

The examinations are open to *any* student, whether or not he has pursued a formal course of study, but they are intended primarily for those who have completed an Advanced Placement course in the subject concerned. The fees are five dollars for registration and eight dollars for each examination taken, payable at the time of the examinations. In most instances these fees are paid by the student, but they may be paid for him by his school board or by any other agency that desires to do so. The school administers the examinations, retaining from the fees paid the sum of five dollars plus one dollar for each examination given, in compensation for costs and as an honorarium. The completed examinations are mailed to College Board Advanced Placement Examinations, Box 592, Princeton, N.J., together with a form, to be filled out by the appropriate high school official, describing the course completed by the student and indicating whether, in the high school's judgment, he is deserving of college credit for his work. The examinations are then read and graded by committees of college and high school teachers, appointed by the Educational Testing Service. The grades are: 5—high honors, 4—honors, 3—creditable, 2—pass, 1—fail. In July the student's paper with the grade given by the committee, and the descriptive form and recommendation submitted by the school, are sent to the college of the student's nomination, which determines what credit or placement is to be allowed him. Finally, in September, the grade or grades earned by the student on the examinations he took are reported to the school.[5] The examinations have a double purpose: first, to test the student's mastery of the subject in question; and second, to ensure that the work of the courses has been kept at an appropriate "college" level. Since the examinations are prepared by high school and college teachers together, they effectively protect the interests both of the school and of the college.

As for the Advanced Placement courses themselves, they may be organized in any way that is in accord with the facilities and policies of the school itself. The Program lays down no requirements as to the number of hours of meeting, the methods of teaching, the texts or other materials to be used, the criteria for selection of students, or the qualifications of the teacher. All of these matters are left entirely to the discretion of the school, which, it is assumed, will wish to do the job well and will best know how to utilize its own resources to this end. Undoubtedly it is best to set up the Advanced Placement course as a regular class, meeting five periods a week with the teacher in the usual way; this plan is to be recommended whenever the school has enough Advanced Placement students in a given subject to make up such a class. But since very few school boards are willing to authorize a high school class of fewer than fifteen or twenty students, it will often happen that enough qualified individuals cannot be found. It should be obvious that Advanced Placement is not for everybody, and not even for all the college-bound. The work requires not only unusual intellectual endowments, but in addition it presupposes a degree of seriousness of purpose and of sheer maturity, which are relatively rare even among the better students in the average high school. Probably not more than the top 5 per cent of the enrollment of the usual school will be capable of handling the work without undue strain and with reasonable prospect of success. Under the circumstances, a school with an enrollment of fewer than five hundred will probably find it difficult to set up a regular class for Advanced Placement; even if only one such class were offered—for example, in English—it is unlikely that all of the putative twenty-five qualified students would be willing to elect it. Furthermore, even in a large school—one, for example, that might be able to find enough qualified students to set up an Advanced Placement class in English or mathematics or both—there are bound to appear, here and there, isolated students who could qualify for such work in one or another of the remaining nine subjects but who could never get together large enough numbers to make up a class. Few schools are able to set up Advanced Placement classes in more than one or two subjects; those that could mount the program with full-sized classes in all eleven are rare indeed.

For the smaller school, and for the occasional student in the larger one, there are three plans, by any one of which Advanced Placement work can be successfully carried on. The first of these involves the so-called "enrichment" technique, whereby the student, enrolled in the regular high school class in the subject concerned, carries on Advanced Placement work through extra assignments and periodic consultations with the teacher. This is an ancient and well-tested device, often used by conscientious teachers for the benefit of students for whom the normal work load of the class is so easy as to lead to restlessness and boredom. It can be, and has been, applied with excellent results to Advanced Placement work. The only special requisite is that the student be sufficiently mature to understand that the extra work assigned to him is an educational opportunity and not a penalty for being bright.

The second plan, often called the "seminar" or "tutorial" plan, envisages the formation of a small group of students meeting during after-school hours or on Saturdays, the number and length of such meetings being determined by the immediate circumstances. In most instances the hours of meeting would not run to more than two or four a week, and accordingly much must be left to the energy and initiative of the students themselves. In many instances, too, such after-hours classes cannot carry high school credit or receive grades; this lack of the usual tangible rewards for hard work imposes an even greater demand for purposefulness on the part of the student. Strangely—or perhaps not strangely at all—such groups have often shown an enthusiasm and industry far greater than that to be seen in regular classes; perhaps the special nature of the class and the feeling of closeness to the teacher more than compensate for the inconvenient hours and for the lack of credits and grades. It may even be that for the truly superior student credits and grades are a sword of Damocles, the removal of which allows him to concentrate on his real purpose of learning something. The chief disadvantage of this plan is the extra burden that it places on the teacher, who nearly always must give his time and energy, both for the class itself and for the necessary preparation, reading of papers, etc., without compensation and without reduction of his regular teaching load.

Finally, the third plan is that of independent study; the teacher lays out a work plan for the student, sees that he knows what is to be done, where the appropriate materials are to be found, etc., and, so to speak, turns him loose to do the Advanced Placement course on his own. Periodic consultations are held to make certain that the student is keeping up with the work, doing it competently and with understanding, and not wasting his time wandering down intellectual bypaths. The independent study plan has many merits. First, it can be used in any school, regardless of size. The pursuit of Advanced Placement courses by independent study provides the small high school with at least one effective answer to Conant's strictures; here, contrary to his discouraging remarks, is something that the small school can do for the academically talented student.[6] All that is needed is one student, able and willing to do the work, and one teacher, able and willing to direct it. Few indeed are the schools that do not have on their staff at least one such teacher; even if Advanced Placement can be offered only in that one teacher's subject, and only to an occasional student whose talents happen to run to that subject, educational progress and improvement will be effected; student, teacher, and school will all benefit. Some limitations may be imposed here in small schools because of the lack of laboratory space and equipment for the sciences, reference materials for history, and facilities for oral practice in the modern foreign languages. Ingenuity can often compensate for the first, community or private libraries for the second, and a resourceful teacher for the third. But of all the subjects offered under Advanced Placement, the two most important, from the point of view of the student's educational progress, are English and mathematics, and these are precisely the subjects that require the least in physical equipment. Paper, pencil, and book serve the mathematician; the English teacher's book problem has been solved by the cheap paperback edition.

The second advantage of the independent study plan is its simplicity and flexibility. It requires no special scheduling, either during the school day or after hours; it can be pursued with or without the reward of credits and grades; consultation between teacher and student can be arranged at the convenience of both and need be no more frequent than the particular circumstances demand. In effect, it requires nothing more of the school, administratively speaking, than that the student be released from the usual school routine for enough time to enable him to complete the work and that he be allowed certain privileges, in the use of the library or laboratory, that are not open to other students. Of all the plans for Advanced Placement, it probably makes the fewest demands on the school and on the time and energy of the teacher.

Independent study has one final advantage that must not be overlooked: it puts the learning process squarely up to the student himself. In addition to mastering his subject, he must learn to organize his work, budget his time, use library and laboratory, and even devise his own problems, all with a minimum of supervision and direction. For the development of sound study methods and habits, for practice in critical thinking, and for opportunity to work originally and creatively, few pedagogical devices are as productive for the truly gifted student as being thus thrown on his own resources. It is painfully obvious that not many students can muster the degree of self-discipline that independent study requires; those who can will have gained thereby the most valuable qualities that they can take with them to college, other than sound mastery of subject matter.

There is one further plan for Advanced Placement work that is sometimes feasible when the number of qualified students in any given school is too small to permit the formation of a class. This is the co-operative plan, by which several such schools band together to establish an Advanced Placement class, or classes, at some centrally located institution—usually one or another of their own number.[7] The primary requisite for this plan is, of course, that the schools in question be within easy reaching distance of each other so that movement of students to the central point and back again to their home schools will not be too time-consuming or expensive. Appropriate financial arrangements between the school districts will also have to be made.

Finally, for schools located in communities where there is an established institution of collegiate level, it might be possible to work out an exchange plan for Advanced Placement similar to that now in effect between Allderdice High School, Pittsburgh, Pa., and Carnegie Institute of Technology. Here, college and high school teachers actually trade places for the academic year, the college teachers taking over Advanced Placement courses in the high school, and the high school teachers taking on sections of the appropriate freshman college classes. This plan is of particular merit from the point of view of the teacher: it gives the college professor a good hard look at the high school and its problems—a look that has been far too long eschewed by the faculties of liberal arts—and it gives the high school teacher direct experience with college level work, experience that should be invaluable to him in conducting future Advanced Placement classes in the high school. Such exchange plans are almost bound to be of the greatest value in bringing school and college closer together and in re-establishing the educational continuum, so badly interrupted for many years, between our "lower" and "higher" schools. The greatest obstacles to the exchange are the salary differential and the difference in teaching load that exist between school and college.[8]

Once the school has determined which of the possible plans for Advanced Placement is best suited to its own situation, the first step is to obtain the *Advanced Placement Program Syllabus*.[9] This brochure contains individual syllabi for each of the eleven subjects; they are models of precision and clarity; they set forth in unmistakable terms the aims and objectives and the range of subject matter which the course must cover if it is to be successfully and profitably pursued. Since the syllabi were prepared by a cooperating group of high school and college teachers, they will be found to take due account of the exigencies and limitations of high school instruction, as well as of the need for keeping the course on a truly "college" level. In general, textbooks and methods of instruction are not prescribed, nor do the syllabi lay down a set of lesson plans or a systematic scheme that must be followed. Rather, all these matters are left, as they should be, to the school and the teacher to choose and devise according to their own lights. The simplicity and clarity of the syllabi make it next to impossible for the school to be in any doubt as to the scope and aims of the course. If the school should wish help beyond what is to be found in the syllabus, this can be obtained by writing to the director of the Advanced Placement Program,[10] who in most cases will forward the request to the Program director for the particular subject involved. This Program director will be able to make suggestions about textbooks, methods of instruction, and the like, and will also be able to supply the names of institutions, both on the college and high school level, which have been involved in the Program and would be willing to offer assistance. Since high schools that have had the Program in operation are almost unanimously enthusiastic about it, help will nearly always be available from them; permission to visit Advanced Placement classes and to discuss some of the problems they raise can readily be obtained.

It cannot be overemphasized that the Advanced Placement course must be carefully formulated and planned before any attempt is made to put it into operation. Schools that have successfully pursued the Program have given at least a year to planning and formulation. It should be remembered that Advanced Placement looks toward college credit for the student who participates in it; in addition, it promises him more than the usual intellectual adventure and progress. Disappointment on the first score is bound to occur occasionally, for not all Advanced Placement students will obtain a high grade on the national examination and not all colleges will accept the course and its accompanying examination for college credit, no matter how high the student's grade. Disappointments on the second score are bound to occur too; it is impossible to please everybody, and there are bound to be students who feel that the course did not live up to their expectations or that it was too difficult or demanding. Students' complaints, like the familiar poor and taxes, are always with us, and the experienced educator has long since learned to live with them. Serious disappointment, whether to school or student, is best obviated by careful planning, but no school should be unduly discouraged if the first round of Advanced Placement is less than perfectly successful.

After preliminary survey and examination of the Program, the next logical step would be the selection of the subject or subjects with which the school can best inaugurate Advanced Placement work. Since the Program involves a good many problems of staffing, library and laboratory facilities, selection of students, and even of such purely administrative problems as scheduling, it is probably best that except in rare cases only one subject be chosen to begin with; once this has proved itself, others can be added as circumstances permit. It can be stated as a nearly universal rule that an Advanced Placement Program should be started with that teacher who is best qualified for the work and most ready and willing to undertake it, regardless of which one of the eleven subjects he teaches. In a small school this procedure is virtually mandatory; even in larger schools, in which there may be several qualified teachers, the factors of readiness and willingness will commonly dictate the choice of one. It is a truism that any course stands or falls with its teacher; this is particularly true of Advanced Placement, which makes far heavier demands on the teacher, both in mastery of subject matter and in pedagogical skill, than does the ordinary high school course.

In many cases, then, the choice of the inaugural subject may be an easy one; this or that teacher stands out as eminently qualified, and the Program begins with him and his subject. Still, the school may wish guidance in the choice of subject—a ranking, so to speak, of the eleven in some order of importance and practicability. For although all eleven are of unquestioned value, and none, on theoretical or philosophical grounds, may be said to be more important or better than any other, practical considerations require that some order of priority be established between them. The question "Where had we best begin?" is both inevitable and legitimate. Any such list must be arbitrary and subjective and is always subject to variation because of local considerations; with this caveat by way of preface, I shall attempt to list the subjects in an order of importance that I trust will seem at least sensible and practical, if not universally defensible.

If it be kept in mind that Advanced Placement is, first and foremost, a college preparatory program, the main purpose of which is to equip the talented student with the knowledge and skills that will best enable him to take advantage of the educational opportunities that the college offers him, then English will emerge, almost automatically, as the most important and critical of the eleven possible subjects. College education is, always has been, and probably always will be primarily "book" education; the student does the vast bulk of his learning by reading. The individual who enters college with well-developed skills not merely in perusing and absorbing but in critically examining a text, with wide experience in many kinds of literature, and above all with a *delight* in reading born of careful, thoughtful direction, is the one best qualified to make his way through the curriculum with satisfaction and profit. If, in addition, he is capable of expressing himself fluently both in writing and in speaking, he is almost certain of success. By contrast, the student who is weak in these areas is equally certain of trouble, no matter how bright he may be. English is a complex subject involving many different skills and aptitudes; furthermore, except in such purely mechanical matters as syntax, spelling, punctuation, and the like, it is not by nature a "structured" subject; its study does not fall readily and easily into a graded series of lessons, one depending logically on another. Mastery of the arts of reading and writing is to be achieved, even by the gifted, only through endless practice; yet no other mastery is so central to the whole educational process. If the school elects, as most will, to initiate the Advanced Placement Program with work in just one subject, and if a properly qualified teacher is present, that subject should certainly be English.[11]

After English, the second choice might well go to mathematics. The past twenty-five years have seen this subject rise from a relatively humble place in our educational system to the point at which it has become pivotal in countless ways. The intimate connection between mathematics and science should always have been obvious and now is indeed so; mathematical reasoning has found its way into sociology, psychology, economics, business, and national defense. Its frontiers are literally as far away as the stars; its specialized topics are so distant from each other that a specialist in one area can scarcely converse with his colleague in another. A great deal has been said in recent years of the importance of giving students an understanding of science; it might be equally wise to suggest that they gain a basic comprehension of mathematics, for mathematics is the key to science.

From all this, it would appear that mathematics ought to be given a consideration at least equal to that of English in the matter of establishing Advanced Placement courses. Ideally it probably should, but even mathematicians must be competent readers and writers before they can do much studying of mathematics; they will do their learning out of books too, and the books will not be entirely filled with mathematical formulae. However, there is one simple but effective block to the primacy of mathematics in the educational scheme, and this is the fact that it depends heavily upon natural aptitude. Why some people take to mathematics like the proverbial duck to water, while to others it remains a forever baffling mystery, is a problem for the psychologists to solve. Perhaps Plato was right when he said that individuals who display natural aptitude for mathematics must be remembering it from a previous existence. Plato was quite serious when he said this; we in our colossal wisdom may find his remark amusing; the educationally important fact is that students do differ widely and dramatically in their aptitude for mathematics, the talented no less than the dull. No talented student can afford to omit any opportunity to perfect his command of English; as for mathematics, many are simply unable to do any such thing and must content themselves with the barest minimum of experience and understanding. Mastery of English is needed by all, of mathematics only by some; for this, if for no other reason, mathematics should probably take only second place in the initiation of Advanced Placement work. By the same sign its claim to priority second only to that of English is very strong, for the student who *is* talented in mathematics should never be held back, if any way can be found to allow him to proceed at his natural pace. He needs this for his own personal satisfaction, and society has great need for his services.[12]

Next in order after mathematics come foreign languages. The reasons are quite similar to those that govern mathematics: first, the need to make provision for the dramatic difference in ability between talented students who have an aptitude for language and those who do not; second, the current position of our country in international affairs, which makes it more necessary than ever before for the schools to turn out people conversant with at least one language other than English. The linguistically talented, like their mathematical counterparts, should be encouraged in every possible way to proceed as rapidly as they can to mastery, both for their own personal satisfaction and for the benefit of the community.

In point of fact, the thorniest question that the school must answer is "Which language?" Not many schools, even in their ordinary courses, can offer instruction in more than one or two languages; very few, indeed, would feel it possible to arrange Advanced Placement work in more than one. There are few, if any, sound logical grounds upon which to choose one language rather than another, whether for Advanced Placement or for the regular high school work; no one language is any better than any other from the purely linguistic point of view; culturally speaking, every major language, ancient or modern, has a rich and varied literature and carries with it a valuable cultural experience. The choice of that foreign language (or languages) in which the school will offer Advanced Placement work might well rest upon such expedient considerations as the availability of a particularly adept teacher, the demand of the students, or the wishes of the community. It should be remembered that the student's linguistic experience will not be limited by the offerings of the high school; students eligible for Advanced Placement will presumably go on to college, where they will have ample opportunity to learn languages other than the one or two they learned in high school. Every high school that can do so should certainly offer Advanced Placement work in at least one foreign language; the choice remains a local problem, and any attempt to set up a priority as between Latin, French, Spanish, and German, on other than expedient grounds, is bound to generate more heat than light. If the school is fortunate enough to be able to offer Advanced Placement in more than one language, the choice ought certainly to be dictated by the student's preference; the linguistic experience gained by him in pursuing any language to this level will be valuable in its own right, whatever the language chosen.

As for the fourth place in the series, the honors had best be divided between social studies (i.e., history) and the sciences. On the surface it would appear that science ought to take precedence; there has been a great deal of discussion recently of the importance of science as an element in the curriculum at all stages, and it is certainly obvious that no talented student, regardless of his special predilections, should be allowed to omit science from his program of study, particularly in the high school. Whether this also means that science is an appropriate subject for Advanced Placement is quite another matter. In many high schools an immediate obstacle to college level science courses is the lack of necessary supplies, equipment, and laboratory space. These deficiencies are often difficult and expensive to remedy, and it is entirely understandable if a school board should hesitate to authorize such heavy expenditures for the benefit of a small number of students. Arguments about the nation's need for scientists and engineers have their weight, of course, and certainly no unusually able student for whom science is the career of choice should be prevented from moving as rapidly as possible toward his goal. Ingenuity, as I remarked earlier, can sometimes supply a deficiency in equipment, and occasionally a public-spirited industrial concern can be persuaded to help. The truly gifted science student, too, is often by nature a lone worker, who, if he is sufficiently mature and responsible, can pursue Advanced Placement study by himself at odd hours and with a minimum of supervision.

Another obstacle to the Advanced Placement Program in science is raised by the fact that most high school teachers feel it imperative to give the Advanced Placement course as a *second* year of study in the science in question. This was not the intent of the organizers of the Program, who meant to permit the talented student to omit the usual introductory high school course and proceed at once to college level work. Advanced Placement courses in English, mathematics, and the languages, because of the preparatory study required, fall almost inevitably into the twelfth grade; it was not felt that this need be the case with the sciences, for which no special preparatory work, other than in mathematics, was either required or expected. There is no reason, empirically speaking, why Advanced Placement biology may not be given in the tenth grade, chemistry in the eleventh, and physics in the twelfth; the mathematics needed for the latter two would normally have been completed in time, especially when it is recalled that students talented in science are almost without exception also well-qualified for mathematics and may even be ahead of the normal sequence by reason of having had algebra in the eighth grade.

The difficulty with setting up Advanced Placement science as a *second* course lies in the fact that it interrupts and dislocates the normal high school program, making it difficult for the student to arrange other necessary courses around it; further, in virtually no case will he be able to complete more than one Advanced Placement science course. However, the institution of Advanced Placement in science as a second year seems to be nearly universal, and no doubt the schools have sound reasons for their practice in this respect. The difficulties that it raises may be considerably alleviated by the expedient, now being more and more widely adopted, of placing biology in the ninth rather than in the tenth grade, and by the practice, already much in favor, of permitting well-qualified students to elect algebra in the eighth.

It has been suggested, albeit with some hesitancy and uneasiness, that many high schools might do well to leave science instruction, except for the regular introductory work, to the colleges, which in general are better equipped, both in laboratories and in staff, to handle it.[13] This would appear to fly in the face of popular demand, which is forcing the study of science down even into the elementary schools. In addition, it may seem to cast a completely undeserved slur on the capacities and abilities of the high school teachers of science. Certainly no such slur was intended; as for popular demand, it needs to be carefully examined for signs of the lack of information that so often misleads even the best-intentioned among the critics of the schools. It may well be that, except in schools that are unusually well-equipped for scientific study, the talented science student would do best to prepare himself as thoroughly as he can in mathematics, English, and the foreign languages, since all of these will be needed for his further work. Basic preparation of this sort will stand him in better stead than "advanced" science courses of questionable precision and thoroughness.

In the case of American and European history, the two branches of the social studies in which Advanced Placement is available, the chief obstacle is likely to be the high school library, which rarely possesses the reference materials that are essential to college level courses in these subjects. Sometimes community or private libraries can supply the deficiency; sometimes the school board can be persuaded to provide the necessary books.[14] Once this obstacle is overcome, the history courses are admirably adapted to the needs of the talented high school student, for whom history opens up endless opportunities for investigation, discussion, and debate. Full of controversial figures and topics, and at the same time demanding constant exercise of judgment and objectivity, it is a splendid training ground for lively minds.

It is perhaps less essential, from the strictly practical point of view, than English, mathematics, or the foreign languages, but its educational value for the student of genuine ability and intellectual curiosity is as high as, if not higher than, that of any other subject available under the Advanced Placement Program.[15] As in the case of the sciences, there is no need to put *both* Advanced Placement history courses in the twelfth grade; one may be offered in the eleventh and the other in the twelfth.[16]

The question of the grade level at which Advanced Placement is to be offered suggests consideration of the ways in which it may be fitted into the regular high school program and of how elaborate the program need or ought to be. Here, as in all other aspects of the work, the question may be answered entirely in terms of the resources of the particular school involved. Generally speaking, Advanced Placement may be either superimposed on the existing high school program, without any radical change in the latter, or it may be organized as the terminal point of a series of preparatory or "feeder" courses, thus creating a separate program running over several years. The "superimposed" type of Advanced Placement course enables the work to be initiated as soon as preliminary planning is complete; the "separate program" type means that actual Advanced Placement courses will be begun only after a group of students has completed the required preparatory sequence. Either plan is possible, and both may be used concurrently.

The "superimposed" Advanced Placement course is much the simpler and more flexible of the two, and is probably the only kind that could be arranged in a small school or for the occasional isolated student in a larger one. Under this plan the school selects from its regular classes those students who appear qualified to do college level work, and offers them the opportunity to do so in the following year. If, for example, in the eleventh grade college preparatory English class, one or more students should demonstrate unusual aptitude for the subject, they might be permitted to take Advanced Placement English in the twelfth grade in place of the regular senior English course. The same scheme could be applied to mathematics, the unusually adept students in the eleventh grade class being chosen for Advanced Placement mathematics in the twelfth grade. In the languages the scheme is equally applicable, except that since few high schools offer more than two years in any language, the selection of those capable of Advanced Placement may have to be made from a second-year rather than from a third-year class, and their college-level work may involve "skipping" a year of regular instruction. In all of these subjects it is clear that the students will not have had all of the formal preparatory work for a college-level course; in some instances the student will have remedied this deficiency by voluntary, independent study of his own—interested by reason of his natural proclivities, he may have gone far beyond the regular required work of his classes. In other cases the gap can be at least partially filled by a program of study to be completed by the student during the summer preceding his enrollment in an Advanced Placement class.

The "superimposed" scheme is also applicable to the sciences and to history; the chief difficulty in these subjects arises from the fact that there is no *one* class from which candidates for Advanced Placement may be readily chosen. If Advanced Placement in science is organized as a *second* course in the science in question, students can of course be selected from the first-year course. Otherwise, candidates for Advanced Placement physics may sometimes be located in the chemistry or mathematics classes, and for chemistry in biology or, again, mathematics. For biology itself, the so-called "general science" course makes a possible hunting ground. In the case of history, students for Advanced Placement in European history may be selected from the regular class in American history, or vice versa; the great importance of reading ability in the study of history also suggests English classes as a source of candidates.

The chief merit of the "superimposed" Advanced Placement course, apart from its flexibility, lies in the fact that it neither disrupts the regular series of high school classes nor requires any extensive reorganization of the school's normal program. The school offers Advanced Placement work in this or that subject; when the student reaches the appropriate point in his schooling and is adjudged eligible, he elects the Advanced Placement course in lieu of a regular high school course in the same subject. Its chief demerit is that it nearly always involves some "skipping" and is therefore likely to be successfully pursued only by the student who has studied on his own, or comes from a home that is unusually rich, culturally speaking, or has other special and unusual talents.

The school that is large enough to do so is certainly well-advised to set up a series of preparatory courses, leading to Advanced Placement, and to inaugurate the program by choosing from among the entering ninth grade students those who appear qualified to pursue work more demanding and thorough than that provided by the regular high school classes. These students are then placed in a special section of the subject in question. At the end of the year this section is again canvassed, and those who have pursued the work competently are placed in a similar section for the second year, and so on until the point is reached at which Advanced Placement may be elected. In both English and

mathematics this means a series of three Advanced Placement preparatory courses, first in the ninth, then in the
tenth, and then in the eleventh grades, with the Advanced
Placement course itself coming in the twelfth grade.[17] Provision must of course be made to permit the withdrawal from
the special sections of those who are unable to keep up with
the work. Similarly, allowance must be made for "late
bloomers," who failed to be selected in the beginning, to
join the special sections in a subsequent year. Whether membership in Advanced Placement *preparatory* sections should
be mandatory or voluntary must be decided by each school
for itself in the light of local conditions and its own policies;
both plans are in use. It would appear, however, that the
Advanced Placement course itself should be elective in all
cases; it seems improper to *require* the high school student
to go beyond the limits of the high school curriculum unless he wishes to do so.[18]

In the foreign languages it is scarcely ever possible to set
up a series of Advanced Placement preparatory courses
such as those in English and mathematics, simply because
even in the largest schools there are rarely enough students
in any *one* of the four languages to permit the formation
of the required special sections. Even if there were enough
students in the first year, enrollment in the foreign languages
has a distressing tendency to drop markedly at the end of
the first year and precipitately at the end of the second year
of instruction; whether Conant's insistence on four years in
one language for all talented students will effect a real
change here remains to be seen.[19] It may well be that special
preparatory sections, although certainly desirable, are less
necessary in the foreign languages than in English or mathematics. Few high school subjects lend themselves so readily
to independent study as do the languages, and in few is

special talent so quickly and easily recognized; the potential Advanced Placement student can be singled out almost at once and set to work either by himself or at tasks supplementary to the regular class work. A linguistically gifted student can in this way prepare himself to do Advanced Placement work by the end of his third or even his second year of study. Probably the most important consideration here is that *some* method of acceleration be provided for the student who learns languages quickly and easily, and that such students be urged to aim at Advanced Placement work. Nothing is more likely to kill their interest than the slow pace of the usual high school language class and the very sketchy command of the language that is its goal; an opportunity to prepare for and complete an Advanced Placement course offers both rapid progress and the goal of real competence.

As for the sciences, the schools themselves, by their practice of setting up the Advanced Placement course as a *second* year of the science in question, have virtually solved the problem of preparation, at least for biology and chemistry. A possible series of preparatory courses for Advanced Placement biology consists of one year of general biology and one year of chemistry; [20] that for Advanced Placement chemistry might be successful completion of the regular high school chemistry course, plus, it is to be presumed, the required proficiency in mathematics.[21] The problem in physics is somewhat different, since this is practically always a twelfth grade subject and a second course is therefore next to impossible. Since the prime requisite for physics, and especially for Advanced Placement physics, is competence in mathematics, the series of special sections preparing students for Advanced Placement mathematics might serve double duty as a preparation for Advanced Placement physics. In any event, the relatively small enrollment in any one science virtually precludes the setting up of a series of preparatory special sections like those for English and mathematics; the Advanced Placement science course must in most cases be initiated and remain as a "superimposed" course.[22]

In the case of history, since the study of this subject is not sequential in the same sense as is that of English, mathematics, the foreign languages, and even the sciences, there is little point in suggesting a series of preparatory courses leading to Advanced Placement work in the subject. The possible sources of qualified students have already been discussed; Advanced Placement history, like the sciences, is by its nature a "superimposed" course.[23]

One of the most important problems in Advanced Placement is that of the selection of students. As far as possible, this is best kept an individual matter; the chances of success for the program are greatest if, especially in the beginning, the students are "hand-picked" for it. If the school already divides its students into ability groups, it will be only natural to begin by canvassing the top-level group for possible Advanced Placement students. If there is no ability grouping, students with consistently good records (A's and B's) in the college preparatory subjects afford a sound starting place. Obviously, the student's grades in the particular subject, or subjects, in which Advanced Placement work is to be offered, are a prime consideration. Beyond this, it may be best, especially the first time selection is made, to give considerable weight to the judgment of teachers and advisers; they may miss some good candidates, but those whom they recommend stand a good chance of being capable. Until some more elaborate and objective method of selection can be put into operation, this combination of grades plus teachers' recommendations will serve the purposes of the first "hand-picking" process, and in some schools—especially the smaller ones, where teachers and advisers come to know their students well and where the number to be selected will always be small—may serve quite adequately for some time.

More nearly objective, and certainly better for the long-range operation, is a selection based on tests such as the Otis and Binet, the Differential Aptitude Tests, the College Board SAT, PSAT, SQT, etc.[24] The immediate problem, when these and similar tests are used, is to determine the cutoff point at which selection of Advanced Placement candidates is to begin. It is impossible to lay down any fixed rule here; each school will have to determine for itself where the cutoff point is to be. It may be stated as a general principle that only the students whom the tests show to belong to the academically talented group need be given serious consideration. On a national basis this is usually interpreted to mean the top 10 or 15 per cent of the high school population; comparison of the test scores made by the students in a given school with national norms will enable the individual school to tell what percentage of its own students fall within this range. Not all of them, by any means, will be capable of doing Advanced Placement work; the Rockefeller Report, in a section dealing with the program, made reference to the top 2 per cent, again nationally considered.[25] Another rough guide is provided by the IQ figure; most schools hesitate to offer Advanced Placement courses to students with an IQ of less than 120, and some insist on a figure as high as 135. IQ is indeed a very "rough" guide and should never be the sole or even the critical determinant. I have seen excellent Advanced Placement work being done by students whose IQ was reported to me as being a good many points below 120. Percentile ranking and IQ together may be used as criteria for drawing up a preliminary list; when this is supplemented by the reports of teachers and counselors, it should not be difficult to sift out those whose qualifications seem to prognosticate success.[26] In no case should cutoff points, however carefully determined, be rigid; the tests, though excellent, are not reliable enough to be applied without being liberally tempered by experience, direct personal acquaintance with the student, and sheer good will. No matter how selection is made, one factor that demands careful consideration is emotional maturity; the student whose attitudes, interests, and ideas are still childish is unlikely to pursue Advanced Placement work with any real profit to himself or to his fellow students. The consent of the student himself is also of the greatest importance—consent based on as thorough as possible an understanding of "what he is getting into." Parents, too, should be well-informed of the nature of the program and of what it is likely to entail in terms of time and effort; their consent to the participation of their children should be obtained and their co-operation enlisted.

Regardless of what subject or subjects may be chosen for Advanced Placement, regardless of the care with which the course is planned and the students selected, and finally, regardless of the adequacy of such physical facilities as the library, the classroom, and the laboratory, the Advanced Placement course will be exactly as good as its teacher. Not all high school teachers, even among the most knowledgeable and experienced, can handle the work successfully; many who are technically qualified will not even care to try. It is impossible to lay down any objective criteria for the selection of the teacher. Credit hours in subject matter or pedagogy prove little or nothing; advanced degrees are no guarantee of qualification. It is easy enough to say that the "best" teacher on the staff should be given the Advanced Placement class; to find that "best" teacher may be quite another matter, for the teacher who may be "best" for the regular classes may be far from "best" for Advanced Placement.

The first requisite is, of course, command of the subject matter—the teacher must have, so to speak, a "college-level" command of his subject. This does not mean that he must be qualified to hold a position as a professor in a university; it means only that he must be familiar with the material commonly covered by a freshman college course, or, more simply, with the material outlined in the appropriate section of *The Advanced Placement Program Syllabus.* Most teachers who completed a "major" in college in the subject to be taught will have had such a command at one time; whether they may still have it, after years of teaching elementary courses, is another question. Few high school teachers have either the time or the energy to keep up with current scholarship; not many have even been able to keep their knowledge fresh by restudy of materials they once had mastered but have had no opportunity to teach. In general, the well-informed and experienced high school teacher will find that his greatest need is for refresher work of some kind. Sometimes he can do this by private study on his own; his best course is to attend one of the summer institutes on Advanced Placement that are being offered with some regularity by colleges and universities in various parts of the country.[27] These will enable him to renew his familiarity with the more advanced phases of his subject and bring himself abreast of new developments both in subject matter and in method. In addition, the Advanced Placement Program itself provides conferences every summer in each of the eleven subjects; these generally center around an intensive study of the examinations of the current year and provide opportunity for teachers, both on the high school and the college level, to discuss various aspects of the work together.[28] For science teachers, yearlong institutes like those financed by the National Science Foundation afford the finest possible opportunity for advanced professional study;[29] for teachers in the humanities, the John Hay Fellows Program provides a like opportunity for a year of study at a university.[30] Neither of these is intended specifically as training for Advanced Placement work, but they provide precisely the kind of study that is needed. Beyond the necessary command of subject matter, the qualifications for the teacher of an Advanced Placement class lie wholly in the realm of intangible personal qualities. Genuine love of learning, infectious enthusiasm, devotion to excellence that communicates itself to his students, a provocative and original mind, intellectual honesty, and a becoming humility—these are and always have been the character traits that make for a great teacher, and it is a stroke of good fortune to find them all embodied in one person.[31]

A rather more practical approach to the problem is to be found in a consideration of the job to be done. Teaching an Advanced Placement class is no easy task. In the classroom the teacher will be exposed to the searching inquiries of keen and sometimes very impatient minds; he will have to spend more time in daily preparation than for an ordinary class. Even veteran teachers have found themselves spending two or three hours every day on such preparation alone. In addition, particularly in English or history, he will be put to the task of devising subjects for papers consonant with the intellectual level of the class; he will have to assign such papers frequently and to read them with the greatest care. Above all, if he is to keep up with the intellectual nimbleness of his students, he will never be able to content himself with what he already knows about his subject, but will have constantly to broaden and deepen his knowledge and understanding by continual study and reading. In fact, he will be asked to do a more arduous job of teaching than is demanded of his colleagues in a college or university, for as a high school teacher he is responsible for the individual progress of his students in a way that no college teacher is.[32]

All of this demands time and energy, and the high school that wishes to institute Advanced Placement should plan to give to the teachers in the program an appropriate relief from the usual teaching load. At the least, the Advanced Placement teacher should be relieved of one course; if the normal load is five courses, his should not be more than four, including, of course, the Advanced Placement class itself.[33] The ideal load for any teacher in Advanced Placement should probably be three classes. It is a little unrealistic to ask a teacher to handle classes on the college level without allowing him free time for study, preparation, consultation with students, etc., as is regularly done in the colleges.

Such relief from the normal teaching load may be expensive; the courses dropped by Advanced Placement teachers will have to be taught by someone else, and this may require additional staff members. It is at this point that the cost of the Advanced Placement Program begins to make itself felt. How much the cost will be, it is hard to say; the costs will vary greatly from school to school.[34] Certainly an important part of planning for Advanced Placement must be an estimate of its cost to the school; to begin it with an inadequate comprehension of its probable costs, and without an entire willingness on the part of the school board to accept and meet these costs, is to invite trouble and possible failure.

There is one aspect of the Advanced Placement Program that is of immediate interest and concern to administrators, teachers, and students alike. This is the matter of academic credit. The courses are all of college level, and as such should in theory carry credit toward a bachelor's degree on the same basis as do courses transferred from one college to another. To what extent is this actually true—or, to put it another way: what chance does the student have of getting college credit for the work he has successfully completed in a high school Advanced Placement class?

It should be emphasized at the outset that the Advanced Placement Program is not primarily a credit-earning scheme. Its aim is intellectual progress and development for the student; it is predicated on the theory that the able student should not be held back but should be permitted to proceed at the rate and at the level of which he is capable as soon as he is capable of it. Basically, the Program offers him not so much an opportunity to earn credit as a chance to learn more in high school so that he may learn still more in college. Because the courses are broader in scope and more concentrated than ordinary high school courses, they afford a firmer base for college work even to the student who fails to get college credit for them.

As I remarked earlier, the actual granting of credit toward a bachelor's degree for Advanced Placement work is and must remain the prerogative of the colleges, each of which will have to determine for itself what its policy is to be. It is impossible to *promise* any student that he will receive college credit for his Advanced Placement courses, no matter how well he may complete them and no matter what grade he may earn on the national examinations. At the present moment, the policies of the various colleges and universities differ widely in this respect. Some grant full credit toward their degrees for all Advanced Placement courses in which the student received a satisfactory grade on the examination, merely upon transmission of the examination results to the admissions officer by ETS. A "satisfactory" grade in this context means 5, 4, or 3. "Full credit" means that the student is granted the number of semester hours (or equivalent) that he would have earned in the parallel course taken at the college itself. If, for example, the college's freshman English course carries six hours of credit (three per semester), the student would receive six hours credit for his Advanced Placement English course. Others will grant credit in some subjects but not in others. This usually arises because the college in question gives a course which it feels to be unique in character and for which it will not accept a substitute, even from another college. In view of the rapid growth of the Advanced Placement Program, it is no more than fair to ask that the colleges make particular policies of this sort known to the schools. In time they will doubtless do so. In the meantime, a student planning to attend a given college, if he is anxious to know what credit he may receive for this or that Advanced Placement course, is well-advised to write to the college in advance for a statement of policy. Still other colleges are willing to grant credit but require that the student himself make formal application for it, in addition to having his record sent by ETS. Failure to submit such application has caused many students to lose credit they might otherwise have obtained. Here again, the colleges have an obligation to inform the schools of this requirement. The student will be wise to inquire in every case whether formal application is required. Other colleges will grant placement—i.e., exemption from the appropriate college course and permission to take the next more advanced course—but not credit; others grant provisional credit that must be validated by successful completion of the next more advanced course. Some limit the total amount of credit that may be granted, no matter how many Advanced Placement courses the student may have successfully completed, e.g., credit may be limited to a maximum of fifteen or sixteen semester hours. Ordinarily, the student may never expect to receive, *at any college*, more than one full year's credit for Advanced Placement work. Still others refuse to allow either credit or placement under any circumstances. In most instances such refusal arises from lack of information about the Program or is the result of the commitment of the college to a program of study that differs in one way or another from the norm. A great many colleges have no definite policy with respect to Advanced Placement, usually because they have as yet had no records presented to them for evaluation.

In view of this great variation in policy, it is manifestly impossible to predict in any given instance what the student may expect; furthermore, as the Program spreads and becomes better known, the policies of the colleges are constantly changing, almost always in the direction of greater liberality. In general, it may be said that most of the "first-line" colleges—to use an invidious but unavoidable expression—are receptive to Advanced Placement and liberal in granting credit for it; it has been statistically shown, too, that those colleges that receive the largest number of Advanced Placement students are the most liberal in allowing credit for the work.[35] From the point of view of the subject studied, those who present Advanced Placement work in mathematics have the best chance of receiving college credit or placement or both: 60 per cent;[36] for all other subjects the chances are nearly the same: approximately 50 per cent. From the point of view of grades, students who earn a 5 are very nearly assured of credit or placement, and those who earn a 4 only slightly less so; those with a 3 stand about a fifty-fifty chance; those with a 2 are rather unlikely to get credit; those with a 1 have virtually no chance at all.[37]

In point of fact, although these statistics are valid for the whole group of students who did Advanced Placement work, they have little meaning for the individual student; for him the chances of gaining college credit depend immediately and decisively on the college that he elects to attend. In other words, it is unrealistic to tell a group of students who are considering electing Advanced Placement courses that their chances of obtaining college credit are about fifty-fifty; if all the group are expecting to enter colleges that grant credit for all subjects in which grades 5, 4, or 3 are earned, then obviously their chances of credit are far higher than 50 per cent; if all are anticipating going to colleges that refuse credit for Advanced Placement courses, their chances of credit are close to zero. Advice to students in this matter of college credit should be given only individually and in the light of the policies of the colleges to which they intend to make application for admission.

Another limiting factor in the matter of college credit is imposed by the schools themselves. In a great many high schools, Advanced Placement courses are available only at the twelfth grade level and often only in one or two subjects. Even when more courses are offered, schools commonly permit the individual student to elect no more than one or two, except in quite unusual cases. This means that even if the student earns high grades on the examinations and is admitted to a college that grants credit for Advanced Placement work, he is unlikely to acquire more than a few hours of credit toward his degree. The credit granted for an Advanced Placement course is usually the same as that which the student would have earned by taking the parallel college course itself; depending again on the policies of the particular college involved and on the particular examination that the student took, he might expect to get somewhere between three and six semester hours for an Advanced Placement English course, between three and eight hours for mathematics, four and eight for a science course, three and ten for a language course, and so on; for two courses his credit will run somewhere between seven and fifteen hours. If he receives placement but not credit, he gains nothing in semester hours but is exempted from the parallel college course, and if this latter is required for graduation, he may normally expect to be exempted from this portion of the graduation requirement as well. It is easy to see that for the largest number of students, Advanced Placement work is unlikely to result in any material decrease in the number of hours that he must earn in order to acquire the bachelor's degree or in any significant shortening of his college career. In point of fact, experience thus far with Advanced Placement students has shown that the accelerative feature of the Program is the one that interests them the least; although some students may use their advanced credit to enable them to graduate from college a semester or two earlier, most of them tend to view this credit as a block of free time which they may use to take courses that they would ordinarily have had to forgo, or to elect courses more advanced than those usually available to the undergraduate. Acceleration in any real sense is likely to occur only when the student has obtained, by Advanced Placement credit, the equivalent or near-equivalent of sophomore standing upon admission to college.

Taken altogether, it is entirely proper to say that the Advanced Placement Program has resulted in the enrichment rather than in the acceleration of the student's education, both in the high school and in the college. As an accelerative device, it has been of interest chiefly to students whose educational ambitions include study in graduate and professional schools and who must therefore anticipate not four but seven or eight years of college. Any reasonable shortening of this long educational road is certainly to be desired, both for the sake of the student himself and for that of society. It is also well to remind ourselves that the frontiers of human knowledge are now far off, especially in the fields of mathematics and science; the potential scholar or scientist must study a great many years before he reaches the point at which he may begin to do original research. Anything that can be done within sound educational practice to shorten his path will be all to the good.

One problem that persistently plagues both schools and students is that of the grades to be given for Advanced Placement courses. The student, no matter how well-qualified, no matter how sincerely devoted to learning for its own sake, is rarely able to escape concern for the grades he will earn; the conscientious teacher and administrator are equally anxious that the grades given in the school shall adequately and fairly represent the student's achievement. Preoccupation with grades is one of the worst features of contemporary American education and has fostered the growth of the "grade-getter"—the slick, ambitious youngster who studies tests and teachers rather than subjects and has a disturbing way of appearing at the top of our grade curves and scholarship lists, where he garners distinctions and awards that might better have gone to some of his less spectacularly successful fellows. The colleges have done little, if anything, to combat this phenomenon; on the contrary, with more and more students clamoring for admission to their limited cubic footage, they have responded by demanding higher and higher scholastic averages from their applicants, with the inevitable result that high school students hardly dare falter in their quest for good grades. Until educators find measures of achievement and aptitude that will more realistically demonstrate the presence of genuine intellectual prowess, it is worse than futile to blame either students or teachers if they are more preoccupied than they should be with grading systems.

The problem is particularly acute in the Advanced Placement class. The student is asked to master materials more difficult than those presented in the regular high school course; he is thrown into competition with a group composed solely of the ablest students in the school. He is understandably concerned for fear he may earn a lower grade in this class than he might have earned if he had elected to take the regular course. He feels that he may be jeopardizing his rank in his graduating class, his chances of admission to the college of his preference, his opportunity for winning scholastic honors, scholarships, and so on.[38] Any plans made by a school to institute Advanced Placement must include some equitable solution to this problem; otherwise, the school may find its ablest students reluctant or even completely unwilling to elect the courses made available to them.

It should be immediately obvious that there can be no grading "on the curve" in an Advanced Placement class; it is patently unfair to assume that in a highly selective group such as this, a certain percentage must receive A, another percentage B, and so on down to E. A proper set of criteria for selection will guarantee that these are all, so to speak, "A" students to begin with; they should not now be graded in competition with each other but only in relation to their degree of mastery of the subject matter laid before them. To phrase it a bit crudely, the student who cannot keep his performance in an Advanced Placement class on at least the "B" level has no place in the class and should be dropped from it; the final grades for the course may very well be all A's, or all A's and B's. It must be noted that the grade the student receives in the *course* may have no relation whatever to that which he earns on the national examination. The latter will not even be known to the school at the time the grade for the course is given. Credit toward the high school diploma is equally independent of any action the college may take with respect to credit toward its degree. The school is entirely at liberty to grant the student full credit toward his diploma for Advanced Placement courses—in fact, to do otherwise is absurd. The fact that the student may subsequently be granted *college* credit for a course for which he has already received *high school* credit is totally irrelevant to the high school situation, if for no other reason than that the college credit may never be granted.

One way to meet the problem of grades—and incidentally, to help prevent excessive "grade-mindedness"—is to guarantee at the outset that every student enrolled in an Advanced Placement class will receive either an A or a B as his final grade. Any such advance contract must be accompanied by a continuous check on each student's performance; if his work begins to fall below the B level, he must be warned and brought in for consultation with the teacher. If he fails to bring his work up to the required level with reasonable promptitude, he must be removed from the class and enrolled in a regular section of the course. In effect, the guaranteeing of an A or B grade is no more than advance warning to the student that he must keep his work at the required level throughout the year if he is to stay in the class at all; it is emphatically not the promise of a gift.[39]

Even so, as every student well knows, an A is an A, and a B is a B, and neither will carry more weight in such matters as rank in class, scholastic honors, and the like, than the same grades earned in a regular class, unless some further differentiation is made. Probably the easiest and most effective way to solve this difficulty is to "weight" the grades given in Advanced Placement classes by increasing the number of honor points assigned to them. If an A in a regular class carries 4 honor points, an A in an Advanced Placement class might carry 4.5 or 5, or even as many as 6. No doubt a statistical study of the school's records would be needed in order to determine the ratio appropriate to that school; the aim, of course, is to see that every student receives the full reward in academic distinction to which he is entitled for the work he has done, and above all, to remove the possibility of a student's being penalized for having undertaken Advanced Placement.[40]

Another way of meeting the grade problem is to give a double grade for Advanced Placement courses. One of these might be called the "high school" grade and the other the "college" or "Advanced Placement" grade. The former would represent an evaluation of the student's work in terms of the standards applied in a regular high school class; this grade would be used to determine rank in class, honor point ratio, scholastic honors, etc. Presumably, this first grade would almost always be an A or a B. The second grade would represent an evaluation in terms of the Advanced Placement course itself, and indicate the degree of success achieved by the student in mastering the materials he was asked to study. Here the full range of grades might occur, although one would not expect to find many below C. This second grade would be hardly more than informative in character, although it might well influence the school's recommendation to the college in the matter of college credit.[41]

One of the student's primary reasons for concern about his grades is the question of admission to college. The flood of applications that comes to the first-class colleges of the country has made a delicate art of the process of selection: when only one out of five applicants can be chosen, and four out of the five are eminently well-qualified, the admissions officer must begin to draw some fine distinctions. These are often based on something other than grades; nonetheless, grades remain a very important factor, and it is certainly true that unless they are good, the student might as well not apply at all. In any event, whether rightly or wrongly, high school students are generally convinced that the difference between an A and a B may represent the difference between acceptance and rejection at the college of their choice. Faced with the certainty of an A in the regular class and the possibility of a B in the Advanced Placement class, the student can hardly be blamed for making the obvious decision.

Actually, his choice may not be as wise as he thinks, even if the school assigns no special system of grading to Advanced Placement classes. The Program is now widespread and well-known; the competent college admissions officer knows what it involves, and realizes that the student who has been permitted to elect Advanced Placement has already been judged superior. He knows, too, that the student who has accepted the opportunity offered to him has by this very fact demonstrated his real interest in learning, his courage, and his resourcefulness, qualities that any college is delighted to find in its applicants. As any experienced teacher knows, it is these intangible moral qualities that make the difference between a gifted student and a mere "bright boy." I once heard a high school principal say that, for success in education, IQ was less important than GQ ("gumption quotient"). Most college teachers and advisers would agree. To put it somewhat imprecisely, the admissions officer knows that a B in an Advanced Placement class is a better indicator of the kind of student the college wants than an A in a regular class, and that as between two students, both of whom could have taken Advanced Placement, the one who did is a better choice than the one who did not.

Broadly speaking, the admissions officer is as much concerned with the courses the student took as he is with the grades earned in them; rank in class is not nearly as decisive a factor as it once was. If the student's record shows that he consistently chose courses of proven academic worth throughout the high school years, his chances of admission are better than those of the student who earned higher grades but elected less demanding courses. The appearance on the transcript of honors or Advanced Placement sections is bound to weigh in the applicant's favor. *Since the admissions officer will know of these sections only if they are marked on the transcript, it is of the utmost importance that the school use some distinctive sign, such as "H," "AP," or "CL" (College Level), for all honors and Advanced Placement courses, and attach to the transcript a note clearly describing them.* This should be done in every case in which a student has elected and completed an Advanced Placement course, no matter by what plan he did the work, no matter what grade he earned on the national examination, and regardless of whether he intends to ask for college credit.

There has been some speculation both in the schools and

in the colleges as to the possibility that Advanced Placement might become a *requirement* for admission, at least to some colleges. Thus far, no college has made a move in this direction, and none seems likely to do so in the immediate future. If this were to happen, it would be at a time when Advanced Placement work had become so common that virtually all applicants for admission to college would have had at least one or two Advanced Placement courses. Such an eventuality presupposes a major reorganization of both high school and college work; if the Advanced Placement Program proves powerful enough to effect a reform of this magnitude, it will exceed all the hopes and expectations of its founders and its present supporters.

There is one final problem that must be mentioned, since it looms very large in the minds of many educators. This is the fear that Advanced Placement courses may have a deleterious effect upon the student's participation in other school activities, may work against his normal development as a person, and may seriously interfere with his social and emotional growth. On the whole, these fears appear to be quite groundless, if we may rely upon the experience of schools that have had the Program in operation over the past five years. Students in Advanced Placement courses may indeed tend to cut down on the number of extracurricular activities in which they engage, but the talented student may have been engaging in some of these simply in order to occupy his time. The Advanced Placement course now gives him a much more meaningful way in which to use his time and energy, and it is entirely natural and proper that he should limit his outside activities to a point consistent with his new program of study. Complete withdrawal from all outside activities, or even withdrawal from them to a point at which harmful effects may be experienced by the student upon his emotional and social growth, seems to occur with relative rarity among talented students. Years ago Terman pointed out in his *Genetic Studies of Genius* that intellectually talented students tend by and large to be equally talented socially and to be better than normally adjusted emotionally; his findings have never been refuted and are now being substantiated by more recent studies of the behavior of students.[42]

As for the charge that the Advanced Placement Program is undemocratic because it grants a special privilege to a limited group of students, this is rapidly becoming a rather battered bogeyman, whose ghost should be laid to rest. It is no more undemocratic to recognize and reward superior intellectual ability than it is to recognize and reward superior athletic prowess or musical talent. Democracy demands not parity of experience but equality of opportunity; it requires that every individual be given an equal chance for full personal development, for only thus can he adequately and properly serve the society of which he is a member. The talented student who does not have opportunity to join a high-level ability group, an honors program, or an Advanced Placement course is receiving less than his full democratic heritage. These are not "special privileges" granted to a "privileged" class of students; they are the right, and at the same time the very heavy responsibility, of a group of young people whose services to society are certain to be of the highest value.[43]

CONCLUSION

In essence, educational programs for the academically talented are based on individual differences; not all students learn all things equally well or with equal speed and facility, and not all are equally interested in education or care to pursue it to the same level or in the same degree. If we believe, as we say we do, that education in a democracy must give every student equal opportunity to develop his own peculiar talents, then we must give at least as much opportunity to the bright as to the average and the dull. To fail to provide the talented student with every possible encouragement to learn all that he is capable of learning is, flatly and simply, undemocratic; to prevent or discourage him from learning, on grounds of some kind of social egalitarianism, is an ugly caricature of democracy.

There is, of course, nothing new about the doctrine of individual differences. Great capital was made of it by the advocates of progressive education in the early part of this century; coupled with the philosophy of John Dewey, it was used as an effective weapon against classically minded educators, who, with a perverse egalitarianism of their own, could see no reason why the old school and the old curriculum—"it was good enough for father, and it's good enough for me"—should not be good for everybody. Strangely enough, once the progressives had won their major victories, the principle of individual differences was laid aside; in its place came insistence on the social values of education, on the importance of co-operation and teamwork, and on the use of the school experience as training in group living, group working, and even group thinking.

The reasons for this change of philosophy were complex, but at least one of them was eminently practical and is readily discernible. This is the population explosion that took place in the high schools in the first half of the present century; great masses of students descended upon the schools, and, the human race being what it is, most of them were of very ordinary academic ability, were of no original turn of mind, and were far more interested in fitting themselves into society than in leading or changing it. Something had to be done for them, and it is unfair to blame educators if, during the 1920's and '30's and '40's, their attention was riveted on needs and demands that were for the moment far more insistent than those of individual differences and the education of the talented. Moreover, teachers could comfort themselves with a theory—which they shared with the general public—to the effect that bright boys and girls take care of themselves anyway: they will learn what they need to know, no matter what the school does or does not do to assist them. Except for a few voices crying in what they were certain was an educational wilderness, everyone—teachers, administrators, professors of Education, and even the public, insofar as it troubled to observe what was happening—was gladly, busily, and quite naturally absorbed in the problems presented by the new mass education.

Changes had to be made and they were made, not always without friction and ill will. There was much pulling and hauling; there were battles, sometimes quite acrimonious, between schoolmen and laymen, between educational theorists and their practical-minded colleagues, between teachers and administrators; the end result was that peculiarly American institution, the comprehensive high school, an institution unique in the world and probably in history. It represents our attempt to provide an education appropriate for all, so that all segments of our population may be trained to participate effectively in our society, each in its own way. It is an impressive educational achievement; with its dozens of activities and interests, the wonder is not that it has some weaknesses and some injustices and that it sometimes fails of its objectives, but that it operates as well as it does. No one visiting our schools can fail to be impressed with the industry, the devotion, and at times the sheer brilliance with which our high school teachers and administrators set themselves to the task of making this complex institution do its work.

But if the major problem of the early part of this century was the formulation of programs of instruction for the vast mass of students, the major problem facing us now is the education of the superior and the talented. There is no blinking the fact that during the period of growth of the comprehensive high school, the ablest and brightest of our students got very little attention. The old curriculum and the old, standard subjects were still there for them to study; if, as was usually the case, their goal was college, information as to what they had better be learning was readily available from the colleges themselves. The school seemed to feel that it had fulfilled its obligation once it had set up a college preparatory curriculum and provided the necessary teachers.

In defense of this somewhat casual attitude, it must be admitted that young people did get educated; the presence in our country today of brilliant young scientists and scholars, most of whom came up through our public schools during this very period, is evidence of the fact that young people could and did learn what they needed to know. At least we may say that *some* young people did; how many potential scientists and scholars were lost for lack of encouragement and assistance, we shall never know. Mass education has a deadly way of becoming anti-intellectual. One cannot help wondering how many people today are living routine lives and thinking routine thoughts because at some critical point in adolescence their nascent enthusiasm for things intellectual was quenched by indifference or guided gently but firmly into activities in which they might be more likely to find social acceptance and win the approval of their peers.

The advent of the first Sputnik dramatized for the whole country our need for trained minds, for inventive, original, and unconventional thinkers in every field of intellectual endeavor, and particularly in the fields of mathematics, science, and engineering. Much of the response to Sputnik was hysterical; here and there even school people, who should have known better, began to talk of requiring all high school students to study science and mathematics, as if a mass response of this kind were any answer to a problem intimately bound up with the traits and the peculiarities of the individual. From within the teaching profession itself, from the less forgiving of those that had long been crying in the wilderness, came wise waggings of the head and remarks of "We told you so!" Figures of some prominence from various fields and even, Proteus-like, from the sea, arose to denounce the schools for their sins of omission; the "antieducationalists" had a field day.

Fortunately, most of the charges and countercharges that were hurled back and forth at the time have been forgotten, and the hysteria has to a large degree subsided. Soberer looks at our schools, like that of Conant, have reassured us about the soundness of our system of education: it has its flaws, but it is firmly based in good sense and good will, in respect for the individual, and in a genuine love for all sorts and conditions of men. We have nothing to learn from the cold efficiency of statist education. We shall learn far better from ourselves, and there are few things more reassuring about our schools than the genuine desire of our teachers and administrators to do everything they can to improve them.

If society is now demanding that the schools pay more attention to the ablest of their students, it is because this group, and this group alone, properly identified and trained, is capable of producing intellectual leaders, and we have come to realize that without intellectual leaders democracy cannot hope to survive. Educators are as aware of this as are any others among us; in many instances—perhaps in far more than we shall ever know—they had long been acutely cognizant of the fact that the educational needs of our able and talented students were not being adequately met. If we wonder why they did not speak out sooner, we need only imagine how much popular support they would have won in the average American community some fifteen or twenty years ago for any educational program—were it enrichment, acceleration, Advanced Placement, or whatnot—that envisaged the separation of the intellectually ablest students from the others, the diversion to them of the best teachers and the best facilities of the school, and the setting up for them of honors and distinctions that could not possibly be won by the rest of the school population. That all of these things can now be done is due no more to a change of philosophy on the part of teachers and administrators than it is to a consonant change of attitude on the part of the public. Now that there is more nearly general understanding of the immediacy of the problem, we may venture to hope that real educational progress will be made. Our schools have done very well by their average students; they have done at times spectacularly well by those who were below average or handicapped. The establishment of programs specially and particularly devised for our ablest and most intelligent students will make of our high schools the truly comprehensive institutions that we should like them to be.

NOTES

NOTES TO I: ACCELERATION, ENRICHMENT, AND
ABILITY GROUPING

1. Nowhere is this more obvious than at education conferences.
   See, for example, the two TEPS pamphlets, "The Education of
   Teachers: Curriculum Programs; A Guide for Follow-Up Stud-
   ies of the Kansas TEPS Conference, 1959," and "The Education
   of Teachers: New Perspectives; The Second Bowling Green
   Conference, 1959." Both pamphlets are obtainable from the
   National Education Association, 1201 Sixteenth Street, N.W.,
   Washington, D.C. For a simpler but equally cogent example,
   see "Accelerating the Academically Talented," *NEA Journal*,
   Vol. 49, No. 4 (April 1960), pp. 22–23. Conant, *The Child,
   the Parent, and the State* (Harvard University Press, 1959).
2. For typical attitudes, see Passow, Goldberg, Tannenbaum, and
   French, *Planning for Talented Youth* (Teachers College, Columbia, 1955), pp. 10, 38, 41, and 49, and the *NEA Journal*
   article referred to above, note 1.
3. Conant, *op. cit.* (note 1), pp. 1–2.
4. Miriam L. Goldberg, "A Report on Recent Research in the
   Field of the Academically Talented," *NEA Project on Ac.
   Tal. Student*, October 1958.
5. Conant, *The American High School Today* (New York, 1959),
   passim. I do not, however, entirely agree with his definition of
   academic talent (p. 20), which seems to me too restrictive.
6. See NEA and NASSP, *Administration Procedures and Practices for the Academically Talented Student* (Washington,
   D.C., 1960), pp. 34–44.
7. See *Admin. . . . for the Ac. Tal. Student*, pp. 35, 46, and 110,
   and USDHEW, *Your Gifted Child* (Children's Bureau Pub.
   No. 371-1958), p. 4.

8. Harold Gershinowitz puts the case well: "I feel quite strongly that if our organizational structure, be it corporate, governmental, academic, or social, becomes so rigid that we cannot encourage, not to say even tolerate, the innovator and the rebel, we shall have reached the end of real creativity, artistic as well as scientific." (The Harvard Foundation for Advanced Study and Research, "Newsletter" [March 31, 1960], p. 1.)

9. See *Admin. . . . for the Ac. Tal. Student,* p. 115; N.Y. State Ed. Dept. *Letter to Supervisors,* Series 7, No. 6, "The Gifted," p. 2.

10. Cf. Conant, *The American High School Today,* p. 23.

11. Charles Bish shows a quite proper concern with the question: "What will happen if all of us—teachers, parents, and other 'interested parties'—'bear down' at the same time?" (Reported in NEA *Bulletin for Building Representatives,* Vol. 4, No. 2, October 1959.)

12. See *Admin. . . . for the Ac. Tal. Student,* pp. 16–18. For a good description of such a seminar, see Florence L. Elder, "A Junior High School Seminar for Talented Students," *Bulletin of the National Association of Secondary-School Principals,* Vol. 43, No. 247 (May 1959), pp. 95–98.

13. *Admin. . . . for the Ac. Tal. Student,* p. 126.

14. A summary of most of these points of view is to be found in *Admin. . . . for the Ac. Tal. Student,* pp. 54–64, and there is an excellent brief article in *NEA Journal,* Vol. 49, No. 4 (April 1960), pp. 22–23.

15. See *Admin. . . . for the Ac. Tal. Student,* p. 65; Lewis M. Terman, *The American Psychologist,* Vol. 9 (1954), p. 226.

16. See Eli Sobel, "UCLA's Special Program for High School Students," *ICSS Newsletter,* Vol. 2, No. 7 (November 1959), pp. 14–17. See also Terman and Oden, *The Gifted Child Grows Up,* pp. 275, 280–81, and 288. Terman's conclusions were widely disregarded during the heyday of social adjustment; they are now coming into their own again.

17. See Walter B. Barbe, "What Is Enrichment?" *School and Society,* Vol. 86, No. 2132 (May 10, 1958), pp. 222–25; *Admin. . . . for the Ac. Tal. Student,* pp. 83–94.

18. This definition is my own. It is based on observation of what the schools are actually doing rather than on educational theory. I fully realize that, by my definition, acceleration and enrichment could take place concurrently.

19. See NEA and NCTE, *English for the Academically Talented* (Washington, D.C., 1960), pp. 51–57.

20. *Eng. for the Ac. Tal.*, pp. 57–66; *Admin. . . . for the Ac. Tal. Student*, pp. 90–94.
21. E. Grand Rapids High School has had such a summer institute (in science and mathematics) for several years. Originally financed by the generosity of local citizens, it is now sponsored by the National Science Foundation. See also the satellite-tracking program of the Thacher School, Ojai, California: *School and Society*, Vol. 87, No. 2151 (April 11, 1959), pp. 177–78.
22. See *Education for the Gifted* (Yearbook of the National Society for the Study of Education, Vol. 57, Pt. 2, 1958), pp. 222–33. These are elementary school classes.
23. See *Eng. for the Ac. Tal.*, pp. 52–53.
24. See C. W. Woolcock, "New Approach Needed for Gifted," NYSED *Bulletin to the School* (May 1959), p. 330. I think it is time that we questioned "breadth" as an educational doctrine. Too often it simply means either a needless scattering of educational effort or the erection of a series of artificial hurdles which the student is compelled to jump. Requirements intended to prevent overspecialization and to insure basic acquaintance with all major fields of contemporary thought mean very little in terms of real education when the student has viewed them as nuisances to be got through as quickly as possible and with the least possible expenditure of time and energy. For a sensible view that deserves attention from American educators, see J. J. Small, "Developing Superior Talent," *School and Society*, Vol. 86, No. 2132 (May 10, 1958), pp. 219–22.
25. See Delmo Della-Dora, "What Research Says about Ability Grouping," *Mich. Educ. Journ.*, Vol. 37, No. 16 (April 1, 1960), p. 513; James B. Conant, *The American High School Today*, pp. 49–50.
26. See *ICSS Newsletter*, Vol. 2, No. 9 (January 1960), p. 4; *id.*, Vol. 3, No. 2 (March 1960), p. 16. The trustees of the Carnegie Foundation for the Advancement of Teaching say flatly, "It is now becoming generally recognized that some form of ability grouping is essential to effective education." (*Summary of a Discussion by the Trustees of the C.F.A.T.* [reprinted from 1958–59 Annual Report], p. 12.) For a good summary of the question, see "Ability Grouping," *NEA Research Memo* 1958-5 (June 1958).
27. E.g., self-concept, level of aspiration, interest, etc.: see Della-Dora, *op. cit.* (note 25), p. 542; H. B. Gores, "Homogeneous Grouping" in "Boys and Girls with Special Abilities" (re-

printed from *NEA Journal,* Vol. 47 [October 1948]), p. 12; *NEA Memo* (note 26), p. 11. Widely quoted in this connection is D. A. Abramson's article, "The Effectiveness of Grouping for Students of High Ability," *Educ. Research Bulletin* (Ohio State Univ.), Vol. 38 (October 14, 1959), pp. 169–82. Abramson finds no significant difference in degree of success in college, as measured by college grades, between students from high schools with ability grouping and those without. His conclusion is not, however, that ability grouping is ineffective, but rather that no valid evaluation of its effect on the quality of college work can be made until the colleges institute a grouping comparable to that in the high schools. In other words, he has been forced to measure the performance of students in a grouped situation against the performance of these same students in an ungrouped situation, and the data obtained are therefore not conclusive: "Until closer co-ordination is effected between the high school and the college, evaluation of the high school program as preparation for work in specific college courses will continue to be difficult" (p. 181).

28. See *NEA Memo* (note 26), p. 4. For a counteropinion, see Paul Woodring, "Ability Grouping, Segregation, and the Intellectual Elite," *School and Society,* Vol. 87, No. 2151 (April 11, 1959), pp. 164–65.

29. See *NEA Memo* (note 26), p. 4.

30. See Woolcock, *op. cit.* (note 24), p. 330; *ICSS Newsletter,* Vol. 3, No. 2 (March 1960), p. 16.

31. Woolcock, *op. cit.* (note 24), p. 330; Woodring, *op. cit.* (note 28); *ICSS Newsletter,* Vol. 3, No. 2 (March 1960), pp. 15–16; *Admin. . . . for the Ac. Tal. Student,* pp. 76–82.

32. *Admin. . . . for the Ac. Tal. Student,* p. 70. A common variation on this provides that the student be assigned to classes of his appropriate ability level in the academic subjects only, leaving the nonacademic subjects heterogeneous (*id.,* pp. 71–72). See also Jean Fair, "The Talented Youth Program," *BNASSP,* Vol. 42, No. 242 (December 1958), pp. 43–44.

33. *Admin. . . . for the Ac. Tal. Student,* pp. 72–74. Conant favors this type of grouping: *The American High School Today,* pp. 49–50.

34. *Admin. . . . for the Ac. Tal. Student,* pp. 70–71. See also the plan in use at Ann Arbor High School, as described in its *Curriculum Guide.*

35. See the *Curriculum Guide* of Evanston Township High School,

Evanston, Ill., and also that of New Trier High School, Winnetka, Ill.; the Evanston plan is well described by Jean Fair,
op. cit. (note 32).

36. So at Evanston. New Trier has four levels. British schools have
fifteen different "tracks."

NOTES TO II: THE ADVANCED PLACEMENT PROGRAM

1. See, for example, the *Bulletin of the National Association of
Secondary-School Principals*, Vol. 42, No. 242 (December
1958), the whole of which is devoted to discussions of and reports on the Advanced Placement Program.

2. Compare the list, for example, with that proposed by James B.
Conant, *The American High School Today*, p. 57.

3. These are located in New York City at the College Entrance
Examination Board, 475 Riverside Drive, New York 27. The
director of the Program is Mr. Jack N. Arbolino.

4. The unnumbered examinations are presumed to be pitched at
the level of the usual college freshman course in the subject concerned; the numbers, when used, indicate the number of *high
school* years of study that would normally be pursued in order
to acquire the required proficiency.

5. Any school wishing earlier reports of these grades may receive
them upon special request at any time after they have been
sent to the colleges in July.

6. *The American High School Today*, p. 77: "The prevalence
of such high schools—those with graduating classes of less than
one hundred students—constitutes one of the serious obstacles
to good secondary education throughout most of the United
States. I believe such schools are not in a position to provide a
satisfactory education for any group of their students. . . ."
This, I feel, is unnecessarily harsh and has aroused both bitter-
ness and despair among educators faced with the incontrovert-
ible fact that their schools fall below the "one hundred line"
and will continue to do so for the foreseeable future. Conant's
remedy, consolidation, is a sound one, but for many school districts it is a counsel of perfection.

7. Cf. NEA and NASSP, *Administration Procedures and Practices
for the Academically Talented Student*, pp. 22–23.

8. The Allderdice–Carnegie Tech. plan was financed by grants
from the Fund for the Advancement of Education and the A.
W. Mellon Educational and Charitable Trust. For an account of
the plan, see B. J. McCormick, "A College–High School Ad-

vanced Placement Program," *The Superior Student* (newsletter of the Inter-University Committee on the Superior Student, Boulder, Colo.), Vol. 3, No. 1 (February 1960), pp. 21–22. More detailed descriptive material is available from Allderdice High School and from Dr. Edwin Fenton, Department of History, Carnegie Institute of Technology. *Note:* This plan should not be confused with the device of permitting exceptionally able high school seniors to enroll in classes at the collegiate institution itself, as has been done at several places, notably in Los Angeles and in Flint, Michigan. For a brief account of the Los Angeles plan, see *ICSS Newsletter*, Vol. 2, No. 1, pp. 14–17; descriptive materials for the Flint plan are available from Dr. Spencer Myers, Superintendent of Schools, Flint, Michigan. This plan is in essence a variation on the "early admission" scheme; it has definite merits but is not, strictly speaking, Advanced Placement. Cf. James B. Conant, *The Child, the Parent, and the State* (Harvard University Press, 1959), pp. 191–92.

9. Available, at a cost of $1.50, from the CEEB (note 3).
10. See note 3.
11. For advice and assistance in setting up the English course, see pp. 43–44. Teachers may also find it useful to see what others have done. To this end, the syllabus, "Sequential Programs in English for the Academically Talented," prepared by the English staff of Evanston Township High School, and "A Summary Plan of the Advanced Placement Course in English," prepared co-operatively by Allderdice High School and Carnegie Institute of Technology, will prove most informative and helpful. These syllabi are in mimeographed form; the former may be obtained from Evanston Township High School, Evanston, Ill., the latter from Carnegie Institute of Technology. See also *The Advanced Placement Program in Independent Secondary Schools*, published by National Council of Independent Schools, Boston (May 1959), pp. 27–28.
12. For an excellent discussion of Advanced Placement mathematics, see *The Advanced Placement Program in Independent Secondary Schools* (note 11), pp. 31–32.
13. See *Education for the Academically Talented, Summary of a Discussion by the Trustees of the Carnegie Foundation for the Advancement of Teaching* (reprinted from the 1958–59 Annual Report), p. 14. The same point is made by a committee of the faculty of Cornell University in a report to the "Citizens for Good Education," Ithaca School District, Ithaca, N.Y. (Mimeo-

graphed report distributed by New York State Education Dept.)

14. For the type of books needed, see the lists used at Allderdice High School (available in mimeographed form from Taylor Allderdice High School, Pittsburgh, Pa.) and *The Advanced Placement Program in Independent Secondary Schools*, pp. 37–40.

15. Excellent syllabi for both American and European history are available in mimeographed form from Carnegie Institute of Technology. These are among the best that I have seen, since they present the work for the whole year in unit form and thus provide a detailed picture of the organization of the courses in a way bound to be helpful to a teacher new to the program.

16. See the Allderdice syllabi. *Special note:* Advanced Placement examinations are taken at the end of the year in which the course was pursued, no matter which high school year that happened to be. If, for example, the student took Advanced Placement American history in the eleventh grade, he may take the national examination at the end of that year; his grade and the school's recommendation for college credit will be kept on file at the Educational Testing Service until the student is ready to apply for admission to college. The same would be true of tenth grade Advanced Placement biology. Advanced Placement work is open to any student *whenever he is judged ready for it,* no matter what his age or what his grade in school.

17. In a three-year "senior" high school, there would of course be only two such preparatory courses, and the initial selection would have to be made at the tenth grade level instead of the ninth.

18. For a description of the work covered in such preparatory sections in English, see "Sequential Programs in English for the Academically Talented" (note 11) and the *Curriculum Guide* of Ann Arbor High School. For mathematics, see *The Advanced Placement Program in Independent Secondary Schools* (note 11), pp. 31–32, and again the Ann Arbor *Curriculum Guide*. The brochure, *Mathematics for the Academically Talented Student*, published by the NEA and the NCTM, will also prove helpful.

19. *The American High School Today*, pp. 69–72. A good many schools, partly, at least, as a result of Conant's recommendations, are adding a third year to the common two-year sequence and are urging their talented students to elect it.

20. So at Oak Park and River Forest High School, Oak Park, Ill. See also *The Advanced Placement Program in Independent Secondary Schools*, p. 33, where several possible approaches to Advanced Placement biology are summarized.

21. So at New Trier High School, Winnetka, Ill.

22. The Westminster Schools, of Atlanta, Ga., report the development of "a sophomore course in physical science consisting of a semester of descriptive chemistry and a semester of elementary physics." The best students in this course are then permitted to take Advanced Placement chemistry as juniors and Advanced Placement physics as seniors: *The Advanced Placement Program in Independent Secondary Schools*, p. 23. The scheme deserves serious consideration by the schools.

23. Allderdice High School, Pittsburgh, Pa., offers a sophomore (tenth grade) course called "Introduction to the Social Sciences" from which candidates may be drawn for Advanced Placement American and European history. This scheme also deserves serious consideration.

24. These, and many other tests of like character, have become so well-known that listing of them seems superfluous. An excellent section on "Identification" is to be found in the NEA and NASSP brochure, *Administration Procedures and Practices for the Academically Talented Student*, chap. 3.

25. *The Pursuit of Excellence; Education and the Future of America*, Panel Report V of the Special Studies Project, Rockefeller Brothers Fund, Inc. (New York, 1958).

26. For a sensible list of check points, see the pamphlet, *Establishing Advanced Placement in the Schools*, published by the CEEB. This might well be supplemented by a list like the one entitled "Suggested Factors in Selecting A. P. Candidates," which is available (mimeographed) from Allderdice High School, Pittsburgh, Pa. Thus far, the schools seem chiefly to have erred on the side of caution; in 1958–59 less than one half of one per cent of all high school students participated in the program. Many more could undoubtedly do so.

27. A list of such institutes can be obtained from the CEEB.

28. Information about these conferences can also be obtained from the CEEB.

29. In 1959–60 thirty-one universities participated in these institutes. For information, application should be made to the Deputy Director for Teachers' Institutes, National Science

Foundation, Washington 20, D.C. Summer, as well as yearlong, institutes are operated.

30. Application should be made to Dr. Charles R. Keller, Director, John Hay Fellows Program, 9 Rockefeller Plaza, New York 20, N.Y. This program also operates two four-week summer institutes in the humanities.

31. Cf. Passow, Goldberg, Tannenbaum, and French, *Planning for Talented Youth* (Teachers College, Columbia, 1955), pp. 56–58.

32. Very illuminating in this respect are the remarks of a college teacher who undertook high school teaching: see Edwin Fenton, "The Carnegie Tech.–Pittsburgh Public Schools Teacher Exchange," *The Pittsburgh Teachers Bulletin*, Vol. 53, No. 7 (March 1960), pp. 102–4.

33. This reduction was made a condition of participation in the Carnegie Institute of Technology co-operative plan (see pp. 42–43). See also Edwin Fenton, "The Future of Advanced Placement in School and College" (mimeographed, available from Dr. Fenton at the Department of History, Carnegie Institute of Technology, Pittsburgh, Pa.), pp. 6–7.

34. Charles E. Bish, of the National Education Association, has estimated that a good program for academically talented students (not necessarily Advanced Placement) will require approximately a 1.5 per cent increase in pupil cost: *BNASSP*, Vol. 42, No. 242 (December 1958), p. 17.

35. For statistical studies of the credit granted for Advanced Placement in various subjects, see the articles by John R. Valley in the following journals: English: *The English Journal*, Vol. 48 (1959), pp. 398–401; Latin: *Classical Journal*, Vol. 55 (1960), pp. 215–16; modern foreign languages: *The Modern Language Journal*, Vol. 63 (1959), pp. 261–63; history: *Social Education*, Vol. 23 (1959), pp. 330–32; sciences: *The Science Teacher*, Vol. 26 (1959), pp. 399–402.

36. Valley, *The Science Teacher, loc. cit.* Actually the percentage in German is higher (Valley, *M.L.J., loc. cit.*), but the number of students involved is too small to make the figure significant for the group as a whole.

37. These figures represent an attempt to synthesize briefly all the statistics given in Valley's articles, which are now a year out-of-date. Estimates of the percentage for 1959–60 would run from ten to twenty points higher.

38. See *Admin. . . . for the Ac. Tal. Student*, pp. 105–6 and 128.

39. This plan is in effect at Taylor Allderdice High School, Pittsburgh, Pa. For details, see the section "To the Student" in the history syllabus (note 15).

40. The system of weighted grades is in use at New Trier High School, Winnetka, Ill., and is described in the *Guide Book to New Trier*, published by the school. A similar system is in effect at Evanston Township High School, Evanston, Ill., and is described by Jean Fair, *BNASSP*, Vol. 42, No. 242 (December 1958), p. 44. It should be noted that if the school's program includes special preparatory sections for Advanced Placement courses (see pp. 55–56), the weighted grades should also be applied to them.

41. This plan is used at Ann Arbor High School: see the *Curriculum Guide* of that school for complete description. If the double grade were applied (as it is at Ann Arbor High School) to the special preparatory sections, the second grade would have considerable bearing on the student's eligibility to continue in the series.

42. See *Admin. . . . for the Ac. Tal. Student*, pp. 33–35; C. W. Woolcock, "New Approach Needed for Gifted," NYSED *Bulletin to the School* (May 1959), p. 329.

43. See Paul Woodring, "Ability Grouping, Segregation, and the Intellectual Elite," *School and Society*, Vol. 87, No. 2151 (April 11, 1959), pp. 164–65; S. L. Pressey, "Concerning the Nature and Nurture of Genius," *The Scientific Monthly*, Vol. 81, No. 3 (September 1955), pp. 123–29; USDHEW, *Your Gifted Child* (Children's Bureau Pub. No. 371-1958), p. 22. The best and most succinct expression of the idea that I know was delivered by Ruth Strang in a paper written for the American Association for Gifted Children, "Guideposts for Parents of Gifted Children": "The danger of creating an intellectual elite is not so serious as the danger of wasting human resources by failing to help individuals make the most of their abilities. It is the goal of democracy to develop the potentialities of every individual, including the gifted." See also *Admin. . . . for the Ac. Tal. Student*, pp. 13–14.